JOHN DEWEY
and the
ART of TEACHING

To
the many pedagogical artists
we have met and admire, especially
the members of the Grace and I. D. Sedah Society

JOHN DEWEY
and the
ART of TEACHING

Toward
Reflective
and Imaginative
Practice

Douglas J. Simpson
Texas Tech University

Michael J. B. Jackson
Educational Consultant

Judy C. Aycock
Texas Tech University

SAGE Publications
Thousand Oaks ■ London ■ New Delhi

Copyright © 2005 by Sage Publications, Inc.

For information:

Sage Publications, Inc.
2455 Teller Road
Thousand Oaks, California 91320
E-mail: order@sagepub.com

Sage Publications Ltd.
1 Oliver's Yard
55 City Road
London EC1Y 1SP
United Kingdom

Sage Publications India Pvt. Ltd.
B-42, Panchsheel Enclave
Post Box 4109
New Delhi 110 017 India

Printed in the United States of America

Library of Congress Cataloging-in-Publication Data

John Dewey and the art of teaching: Toward reflective and imaginative
practice / Douglas J. Simpson, Michael J. B. Jackson,
Judy C. Aycock.
     p. cm.
Includes bibliographical references and index.
ISBN 1-4129-0902-3 (cloth) — ISBN 1-4129-0903-1 (pbk.)
   1. Dewey, John, 1859-1952—Contributions in education.
2. Education—Philosophy. I. Simpson, Douglas J.
II. Jackson, Michael J. B. (Michael John Brierley), 1943- III. Aycock, Judy C.
LB875.D5J64 2005
370′.1—dc22
                                        2004016440

04   05   06   07   10   9   8   7   6   5   4   3   2   1

Acquiring Editor:	Diane McDaniel
Editorial Assistant:	Margo Crouppen
Production Editor:	Diana E. Axelsen
Copy Editor:	Julie Gwin
Typesetter:	C&M Digitals (P) Ltd.
Indexer:	David Luljak
Cover Designer:	Michelle Lee Kenny

Contents

Preface

This book has been emerging throughout our careers and, perhaps, lives. Our teaching and learning with and from teachers, classmates, professors, colleagues, and students in the United States and Canada have significantly influenced our thinking—and, no doubt, lack thereof, at times—in *John Dewey and the Art of Teaching*. These streams of thought, criticism, and imagination have been slowly working out of our minds and into this book. Yet, from a different slant, ideas for this volume sprang to mind very recently. Springing forth as they did, we cannot help but think of the article "What Is the Matter with Teaching" (LW 2: 116–123)? Dewey queries us, "What can be done to liberate teachers, to free their personalities and minds from all the petty economic, social and administrative restrictions which so frequently hem them in and repress them" (LW 2: 123)? Our subtitle—*Toward Reflective and Imaginative Practice*—is based in part on Dewey's question, a question that still needs to be addressed by administrators, teachers, board members, policymakers, caregivers, and other interested parties.

No definitive answer that fits all situations exists for Dewey's question, of course, but part of the solution resides in the profession, policymakers, politicians, and others in society better understanding and appreciating the importance of teachers becoming more artistic in carrying out our responsibilities. Artists need both form and freedom to do what we are best prepared to do, not pressure and prescription to control our thinking and acting. So, as long as teaching is viewed as a technical or mechanical trade that requires only a minimum of talent, preparation, and freedom, we cannot hope to attract and retain large numbers of highly talented people who enjoy the arts of thinking and teaching—unless, perhaps, we continue to attract a significant number of teachers whose commitment to children and society overrides the repugnance of the subculture of schooling that legislatures and policymakers allow to exist and, at times, help create. But we run the risk of destroying the quality that remains in schools if we continue to exploit the goodwill and compassion of the highly capable and dedicated educators who serve students and society.

We hope this book will act, at least in part, as a small counterforce to the restrictive laws, policies, and practices that emanate from social, political, and educational strongholds that promote the myth that teaching is simple, predictable, and easy. So easy, if we believe the myth, that nearly anyone—excluding, perhaps, those who are emotionally unhealthy or criminally imprisoned—with a university degree and an average IQ can do very well as a teacher. These aggressive voices argue for educational oversimplification at a time when we need to understand the complexities of teaching and need to promote intelligent analysis of the assorted challenges of students and schools. Thus, if we had a subtitle for this work that were sufficiently descriptive, it would be *Toward the Liberation of Teachers from Unimaginative Practices, Policies, Prescriptions, Principals, and Politicians*. This subtitle may sound arrogant, and it might be, if it were not for at least four considerations. First, the content of this work is largely consistent with the reflective thinking and practice of thousands of highly respected and successful educators that we have met in Canada and the United States, not based merely on our own fairly limited experiences and research. Second, there is a growing body of empirical research and reflective scholarship that is consistent with the lived practice and thinking of the outstanding educators that we have come to know and appreciate. This body of reflection and research is available to anyone who will take the opportunity to examine it. Third, the ideas in this work reflect to a sizable degree the thinking of another highly important source of insight, John Dewey, the educational philosopher who is arguably the most comprehensive and insightful thinker on teaching and teachers to emerge in the Americas. Although this is far from being a modest claim, it stands in spite of the dismissal of Dewey's ideas by those who falsely assert that they understand but find little or nothing to appreciate in his philosophy of teaching. Fourth, we are not asserting that the ideas in this brief work are sufficiently powerful to immediately or permanently liberate teaching from the conscious and unconscious forces that seek to make and keep the teacher, as Dewey says, a "mere tradesman" and make the school "a mere machine shop" (Archambault, 1964, p. 201). Pedagogical liberation, like other kinds of functional freedom, is an ongoing process that is based on an understanding of relevant knowledge and conditions and the continuous application of such understanding to the concerns of educators. This volume, then, is simply a tiny step toward liberating teachers so that we can practice the art of cultivating intelligent and caring youth. Again, as Dewey avers, the cultural, political, and professional bondage that still treats the teacher as "a living phonograph" and "a servile rubber stamp" needs to be broken and, ideally, shattered (LW 2: 122).

We deeply appreciate the assistance of the Sage editorial staff, especially Diane McDaniel, who showed an interest in this work and helped to bring the project to the public. Her helpful suggestions and support are deeply appreciated. We also thank the reviewers who critiqued several earlier, somewhat preliminary publications. These earlier works include two articles by the first two authors: "Glorious Dreams and Harsh Realities: The Roles and Responsibilities of the Teacher From a Deweyan Perspective," *Paideusis* (*8*[2], 1995) and "The Multiple Loves of the Successful Teacher," *Educational Foundations* (*12*[1], 1998). Permission to use ideas from these works is greatly welcomed. Likewise, we appreciate the excellent feedback we received from the formerly anonymous reviewers of a previous draft of this book: Ranae Stetson, Texas Christian University; John P. Portelli, University of Toronto; Tony W. Johnson, West Chester University; Jackie M. Blount, Iowa State University; and Joe DeVitis, Georgia College and State University The suggestions we received from these educators were invaluable as we completed this volume.

A special debt is also owed to The Society of Professors of Education for an invitation to the first author to give the Mary Anne Raywid Lecture on "John Dewey's View of the Teacher as Artist." Preparing this lecture widened the scope and depth of our understanding and appreciation of the subject and the insightful ways in which Dewey addresses the art of teaching. Although this book is essentially a new project, these earlier undertakings helped prepare for and shape the thinking in this work. A final word of thanks goes to Xiaoming Liu, research assistant, and Margaret Graham, administrative assistant, College of Education, Texas Tech University, Lubbock. Liu's invaluable suggestions throughout the writing, editing, and proofing of drafts were immensely helpful, and Graham's support in the creation of figures is most appreciated.

Citations? A brief comment about them appears necessary. All quotations from and references to Dewey's writings, with the exception of references to Reginald Archambault's *John Dewey on Education* and Jo Ann Boydston's *The Poems of John Dewey,* are to *The Collected Works, 1882–1953,* edited by Jo Ann Boydston. Published by Southern Illinois University Press, *The Collected Works* is divided into three sets of works, namely *The Early Works, 1882–1898*; *The Middle Works, 1899–1924*; and *The Later Works,*

1925–1953. References to these works are abbreviated, for example, as EW 5: 94 (indicating the material cited or idea noted is in *The Early Works,* Volume 5, page 94). *The Collected Works* allow us easy access to nearly all of Dewey's writings and to have a uniform bibliographical style. We also refer in the text to many of Dewey's books and articles by title so that these particular works can be used if the reader desires. Clearly, we could not have completed *John Dewey and the Art of Teaching* as we desired without the permission of Southern Illinois University Press to quote from *The Collected Works* and *The Poems of John Dewey* and Random House, Inc., to quote from *John Dewey on Education: Selected Writings.* We should note that we have not given a great deal of time to evaluating Dewey's thoughts, situating his ideas historically, or comparing his beliefs with those of his contemporaries and more recent writers. Recognizing the importance of the former, we have raised a variety of questions throughout the work to stimulate the reader to question whether Dewey's ideas are conceptually clear, cogently argued, and well supported. Although we also realize the value of the contextualizing Dewey's ideas if they are to be properly understood and evaluated, we chose another course. Much of what he wrote is current and applicable to multiple periods and contexts. Because of this sense of contemporariness in his writing, we decided to write as if Dewey made his statements this morning, knowing that this can misrepresent his ideas on occasions. This risk may be worth taking in the interest of readability and relevancy. For those who desire a greater understanding of the historical context of his writings, we recommend Jay Martin's *The Education of John Dewey: A Biography,* Louis Menand's *The Metaphysical Club: A Story of Ideas in America,* Alan Ryan's *John Dewey and the High Tide of American Liberalism,* and Robert Westbrook's *John Dewey and American Democracy.*

The third omission—not weighing Dewey's ideas by those of his contemporaries and more recent writers—is unfortunate for a number of reasons. Included among these reasons is the fact that selected discussions of thinkers like William James, Edward L. Thorndike, Mortimer Adler, Lev Vygotsky, W. E. B. Du Bois, Nel Noddings, William Bennett, Jane Roland Martin, Paulo Freire, and Maxine Greene, to mention just a few, would have greatly enriched the readers' understanding of the strengths and shortcomings of Dewey as well as immensely broadened their grasp of the educational issues that confront teachers and society. Our decision not to introduce these educational theorists was based largely on the desire to concentrate on Dewey's theory of the art of teaching and education.

In closing, we want to express our gratitude to the Helen DeVitt Jones Foundation and Texas Tech University. Each contributed to the completion of this volume by helping provide a supportive research environment that extends beyond the customary. If not for the indirect assistance of the former and the milieu of the latter, this project would have been delayed considerably. Actually, it might not have even been started, much less finished. Our enormous debt extends down the corridors, across the university, and into the city.

Douglas J. Simpson
Lubbock, Texas

READINGS

Archambault, R. (Ed.). (1964). *John Dewey on Education: Selected Writings.* Chicago: University of Chicago Press.

Boydston, J. A. (Ed.). (1977). *The poems of John Dewey.* Carbondale, IL: Southern Illinois University Press.

Democracy and Education, (MW 9).

The Early Works of John Dewey, 1882–1898 (5 volumes). (1972). Carbondale and Edwardsville: Southern Illinois University Press.

The Later Works of John Dewey, 1925–1953 (17 volumes). (1989). Carbondale and Edwardsville: Southern Illinois University Press.

Martin, J. (2002). *The Education of John Dewey: A Biography.* New York: Columbia University Press.

Menand, L. (2001). *The Metaphysical Club: A Story of Ideas in America.* New York: Farrar, Straus, and Giroux.

The Middle Works of John Dewey, 1899–1924 (15 volumes). (1982). Carbondale and Edwardsville: Southern Illinois University Press.

Ryan, A. (1995). *John Dewey and the High Tide of American Liberalism.* New York: Norton.

Westbrook, R. (1991). *John Dewey and American Democracy.* Ithaca, NY: Cornell University Press.

About the Authors

Judy C. Aycock (PhD, Memorial University of Newfoundland) is Assistant Dean, College of Education, Texas Tech University. She was a middle and high school English teacher before becoming a professor and administrator at Tennessee State University, Nashville; University of Louisville, KY; and Texas Wesleyan University (TWU), Fort Worth. At TWU, she directed the interdisciplinary program and was named the Ralph and Sue McCann Professor for excellence in teaching. She is the author of a variety of publications, including *Art of the Western World* (Moore Educational Publishers, 2004), *Analysis and Interpretation of Literature* (Moore Educational Publishers, 1998), and *Ethics: Theory and Practice* (Moore Educational Publishers, 1998).

Michael J. B. Jackson (PhD, University of Toronto) lives in Montreal, Quebec, and Vancouver, British Columbia. He is the author or coauthor of numerous publications, including *Educational Reform: A Deweyan Approach* (Garland Publishing, Inc., 1997) and *The Teacher as Philosopher* (Methuen, 1984). He was a professor and served as Chair of the Graduate School of Education at Bishop's University and Head of the Department of Educational Foundations at Memorial University of Newfoundland, where he assisted student teachers and interns as they prepared for their first teaching appointments. In addition, he has taught at several other Canadian universities, including Concordia, Queen's, Mount St. Vincent, and British Columbia.

Douglas J. Simpson (PhD, University of Oklahoma) is Professor, Curriculum and Instruction, and the Helen DeVitt Jones Chair in Teacher Education, Texas Tech University, Lubbock. He is the author, coauthor, or editor of many publications, including *The Pedagodfathers* (Detselig Enterprises, Ltd., 1994), *Recreating Schools: Places Where Everyone Learns and Likes It* (Corwin Press, 1998), *Educational Reform: A Deweyan Approach* (Garland Publishing,

Inc., 1997), *The Professional Development School: A Commonsense Approach to Improving Education* (Sid Richardson Foundation, 1993), *The Teacher as Philosopher* (Methuen, 1984), and *To Serve and Learn: The Spirit of Community in Liberal Education* (Peter Lang, 1998). Once each week, he enjoys teaching students at Phyllis Wheatley Elementary School and discussing historical, ethical, and geographical ideas with them. Since 2001, he has been a visiting professor at the Summer Institute, Mount Saint Vincent University, Halifax, Nova Scotia.

ONE

Introduction

It is difficult always to be a creative artist. I think, however, that we should get on more rapidly if we realized that, if education is going to live up to its profession, it must be seen as a work of art which requires the same qualities of personal enthusiasm and imagination as are required by the musician, painter or artist. Each of these artists needs a technique which is more or less mechanical, but in the degree to which he loses his personal vision to become subordinate to the more formal rules of the technique he falls below the level and grade of the artist. He becomes reduced again to the level of the artisan who follows the blue prints, drawings, and plans that are made by other people.

—John Dewey (MW 15: 186)

If we have taught extensively, we know that effective teaching—teaching that accomplishes the things we desire—is one of society's most complex, challenging, and compelling endeavors. Good teaching demands that we

---

Authors' Note: References to works by John Dewey are from the collection of his works published by Southern Illinois University Press: *The Early Works of John Dewey, 1882–1898; The Middle Works of John Dewey, 1899–1924*; and *The Later Works of John Dewey, 1925–1953*. References to these works are abbreviated as EW, MW, and LW, where, for example, EW 5: 94 indicates that the material cited or idea noted is in *The Early Works*, Volume 5, page 94.

progressively become better educated people ourselves, as well as grow in our understanding of our teaching fields, cultivate our abilities to communicate effectively, and enrich our understanding and effectiveness in guiding multiple social and intellectual interactions. Doing these things—becoming better educated and learning more about our teaching fields, communication, and human interactions—is daunting. No, it is actually staggering in many schools today. In fact, much more is required of teachers. If we are going to positively influence children and youth as maturing, whole people, we will be called on to touch more than their intellectual development; for example, we will need to give attention to their social, emotional, ethical, and physical growth.

The challenge becomes even more intimidating when we see that the teacher is more than a successful classroom educator. She[1] needs, for instance, to be prepared to help the public, caregivers, policymakers, neighbors, business leaders, board members, friends, and politicians better understand the realities of the teaching profession. The advocacy and public relations roles of the teacher increase as the profession becomes more misunderstood, less respected, and regularly belittled in explicit and implicit ways. Of course, she does even more, including serving on school and district committees, volunteering for extracurricular activities, maintaining bridges to parents and guardians, purchasing materials and equipment, and engaging in professional development activities. The list of involvements for professional educators extends into their homes and communities and into organizations where daily and year-long activities and discoveries inform work and provide evidence that teaching is not an 8:00 a.m. to 3:00 p.m. job for nine months a year.

In this volume, however, we are primarily interested in aspiring and practicing teachers understanding teaching and learning. Even this domain, however, requires more than knowledge of one's teaching field and the ability to talk to students. But this particular knowledge and ability is not as simple as many critics innocently imply. If we were to take the time to walk into a classroom of children or adolescents and tell them that we are their substitute teacher, we would soon learn that our perception of teaching as being merely that of imparting information and talking is badly mistaken. If we were to choose to return as a substitute teacher for a few more days, our appreciation for good teaching and teachers would grow immensely, for, as we stated earlier, teaching is a complex undertaking that demands the best artists.

Serving as a substitute teacher for a week, however, would not tell us everything we need to study to become a teacher, much less a professional educator, for the desire to learn while substitute teaching would of necessity be slanted toward ourselves: toward surviving in the classroom, not truly educating students. Indeed, we probably would not even know what educating a person really entails if we have never studied the topic. After passing the threshold of classroom survival, without which little teaching is possible, we would probably shift our focus to simply teaching ideas and information or, worse, merely transmitting facts and figures. Focusing on survival and transmission of information is a problem for more than many substitute teachers: People who are first-year teachers, teachers who have been poorly prepared to teach, and those who have missed thoughtful educator preparation programs are prone to have similar challenges.

Some critics believe that those teachers who have nearly insurmountable problems with students just do not have "what it takes" to be effective educators. Obviously, some don't, but others do after they are appropriately prepared. "What it takes" can be learned: People do. But those who either naturally have or have developed what it takes to manage classrooms are not automatically going to be good teachers, much less professionally informed educators. They have an important prerequisite, but more is needed.

People who genuinely understand teaching realize that it entails considerably more than having knowledge of subject matter and pedagogy and being gifted (whether from nature or experience or study or all three). It also includes a set of understandings, activities, interactions, relationships, ways of thinking, and grounded habits of intuiting based on a broad knowledge of many things, such as society, families, children, psychology, democracy, learning, ethics, community, pedagogy, and forms of inquiry and creativity. This is why the contributions of different kinds of researchers, scholars, and practitioners are needed to illuminate the work of teachers. Because the bodies of reflection and knowledge that inform teachers are growing, we must also. A narrowly focused personal or district professional development plan or program only reinforces the myth that a little training and giftedness make teaching simple and easy and that problems are simple and isolated. Believing that teaching is an unproblematic and straightforward undertaking, then, is one of the most dangerous contemporary ideological errors. More important, it hinders students' learning and limits their lives. As a dogmatic myth, it does not answer critics. It silences opponents by attacking, disenfranchising, and disempowering them. The myth makers welcome the opportunity to discredit their critics, not by a reflective examination of evidence and argument but by ad hominem claims. The myth of the simplicity of being a teacher, therefore, is a serious hindrance to both educating future teachers and advancing the education profession. Rejecting this popular myth is an important step in realizing that the genuine teacher is much different than the stuffer of minds in a small, cramped room.

How do we get beyond this educational myth, this black hole that sucks so many of us into it? Or, in Dewey's words, how can we assist others in understanding that education is "the most complex, intricate and subtle of all human enterprises" (LW 3: 255)? No exit seems to exist if we do not try to get beyond our stereotypes and think carefully about the steady streams of ideas that can overwhelm us. Throwing away the irrelevant and mindless ideas that come our way is crucial. This winnowing takes time and thought, however. Much time is required to discover, test, and apply the reflective and reliable in these streams of thought and, unfortunately at times, non-thought. Our culture, within and outside of schools, cannot be liberated from its myth if we as a society and profession don't appreciate the very possibility of learning much more about teaching. To believe that we have arrived is a sign that we have stopped growing as professionals. To think that there is little or nothing to learn about being a professional is equally deadly. So, we turn briefly to some important attempts to free us from the narrow-minded myth of teaching being an effortless and uncomplicated undertaking.

Some researchers attempt to understand teachers and students by pursuing quantitative and qualitative studies in classrooms and schools. They give us psychological, anthropological, and sociological norms, averages, and trends, as well as close-up pictures of particular cultures, populations, schools, and individuals. Other scholars examine historical, ethical, and philosophical issues to see what has been, why it has been, and whether it should have been or should be now, offering analytical, interpretative, evaluative, and comprehensive insights. Still other researchers investigate the development of the central nervous system, especially the brain, to inform teachers. In addition, they discover information that helps parents and health care workers better prepare each child for more successful learning experiences. Related to this research are the findings of medical and behavioral scientists that help us understand the development of children and youth and, thereby, provide insight regarding human growth and learning. Many other academics contribute by studying the teaching and learning of specific subjects, such as languages, art, mathematics, music, biology, reading, history, and health education. But the best of scholars and researchers can disappoint us if we expect too much—or the wrong things. They can only provide insights, concepts, principles, patterns, schemata, data, and criticism. These contributions are valuable, even essential, but beyond that, they demonstrate that teaching is complex and will always require interpretation by reflective, imaginative, and experimental thinkers and practitioners. They provide us with information sources and illumination that help us become artists if we study them carefully. Artists, of course, are not people who are trained to follow rules, formulae, and directions mindlessly.

Others who study education and schooling, like us, draw from many of the humanistic contributors to try to clarify teaching by studying and creating images and conceptual pictures of teaching. Raising probing questions, for example, is important: What is happening when a teacher has the relevant understandings and uses her mind, and especially her imagination, to turn a so-called dull subject and 30 bored students into a lively, engaged learning community? And why is it happening? Asked another way, what happens when a sterile auditorium is transformed into a theatrical setting? Before moving forward with these questions, we should say that it does not just happen. No way. A great deal of learning, imagination, preparation, planning, and practice is required before the curtains are raised—or the students are engaged and learning.

Images and pictures can help us understand the work of the artist—whether a drama director or a classroom teacher—in the theatre and in the classroom, and both positive and negative images help clarify what we wish to promote and discourage. Think of the earlier depiction of the teacher by Dewey when he compares her to an artisan who "follows the blue prints, drawings, and plans that are made by other people" (MW 15: 186). Will this mental picture attract future teachers? Does the experience of doing what has been handed to or forced on us by others help retain teachers? What about Dewey's image of "a tradesman" who works in a "machine shop" (Archambault, 1964, p. 201)? Who among us wants to be "a living phonograph" or "a servile rubber stamp" (LW 2: 122)? Nothing is wrong, of course, with being an artisan or a tradesperson. Indeed, a great deal is to be admired about being a highly qualified artisan or tradesperson. But teachers, as cultivators of thinking people, have different roles to play and should be creative and reflective as they develop students who exhibit these and other qualities. We do not—or should not—simply implement the plans of others; we have to think for ourselves. Who wants to be seen as a disc spinner or rubber stamp? Maybe there are a few aspiring and practicing teachers who admire these images, but are they the people we want to educate our children and youth? And would they inspire their own students to become immediate learners, much less future teachers?

Our point, we hope, is clear: Some images are repugnant and repel. Dewey's depictions, thus far, fit into this category, and many current mental pictures as well as realities of teaching are largely distasteful to people. Why, we might ask, would anyone with two brain cells want to be a teacher today? No one would. Well, that is not exactly correct. In reality, there is a variety of reasons intelligent, caring people want to be teachers, but they are not attracted to the field because it has a genuinely positive image. Those who have admirable motives want to teach because they love to learn, enjoy being with students, want the best for society, and so forth. Frequently, they are clearly choosing the profession in spite of its image.

So, where does this lead us? To begin with, it tells us that figures of speech—analogies, similes, and metaphors—and literalisms are often used to depict teaching negatively. On the other hand, they enable us to uncover or clarify important dimensions of teaching or being a teacher. Sometimes the images or analogies slip over into ordinary usage, and their meanings are partially hidden or, on occasion, they are interpreted in a literal fashion. The explicit images seem more powerful than the hidden ones, but the implicit or hidden pictures of teaching and the teacher can be influential, too. Their potency may rest in the fact that they represent more than points of comparison: They often contain fundamental and intrinsic insights into the nature of teaching and learning.

Images of the teacher, whether explicit or implicit, figurative or literal, are the focus of this book. More specifically, we examine some of the writings of John Dewey to unearth his thinking on the teacher, teaching, and, to a degree, learning. Other educational thinkers could be studied, from Plato to Maxine Greene. Plato, for example, is famous for his picture of the teacher as a midwife. Helping students give birth to ideas is certainly a vivid image and unforgettable pleasure. Erasmus suggested that teaching is like farming. Cultivating the growth of children and youth, therefore, has become a common way of seeing our work. Rousseau saw the teacher as a person who engages in a very demanding art. And who wishes to deny that teaching is both demanding and an art? Certainly, not teachers, teaching interns, and substitute teachers. Richard Peters believed that the teacher is a guide who initiates the young into forms of knowledge and that we should guide students so that they can join the ranks of those who are on the inside of reading, writing, and calculating as well as of thinking in terms of history, art, mathematics, music, biology, religion, literature, chemistry, politics, government, and physics. John Holt reminded us of similarities between the teacher and the travel agent who helps students plan their educational journeys. Sharing opportunities and options with students, as this analogy suggests, is a wonderful part of teaching. Maxine Greene compared the teacher to a stranger who sees newness and wonder in learning. The teacher invites students to become fellow strangers and to travel with her, in groups as well as individuals, to see or discover the previously unseen, unrecognized, and unimagined. These images, carefully examined, frequently help us understand in part what teaching is, not just what teaching is like.

The stranger, the travel agent, the guide, the artist, the farmer, and the midwife—as well as many other images of the teacher—greet us in educational literature. Many writers appear content with one or two powerful images of the teacher and run the risk of being misinterpreted by anyone who is looking for a simple solution to the challenges of teaching. This is the legacy of the myth of simplicity and, perhaps, a natural tendency. There are already too many seekers of trouble-free explanations, too many people searching for the cure to all educational problems. In fact, there are far too many people in various walks of life who think they have already discovered the panacea for perfect pedagogy and, consequently, set us farther back than they move us forward. We do not want to leave the impression, therefore, that either Dewey or we think that if a teacher becomes a sophisticated educational artist, all of her challenges will disappear, students will be accepted into prestigious universities, and schools, communities, and countries will flourish. Teaching and learning are far more complex and complicated than simply being an imaginative artistic teacher. And so is the overall welfare of a student, not to mention a country. Obviously, however, we think that being an artist in the learning communities of our schools will help enliven and enrich teaching, learning, and schooling in radically important ways. Teaching with cadres of other artists can only extend the learning communities down the hallways of our schools.

David Hansen is a notable exception to the pattern of suggesting that a single metaphor captures the heart of teaching.[2] He noted comparisons between the teacher and, among others, a father, director, monarch, lover, servant, and artist. No one comparison says it all. Nor does any set of analogies provide all of the illumination and wisdom we need. Nor are images enough: Other forms of inquiry and reflection are necessary if we are to have a comprehensive view of the teacher as an artist and a professional who has the knowledge, understanding, skills, and imagination that are required for developing an artistically exciting, intellectually stimulating, and aesthetically satisfying learning environment. Moreover, it is critical that we keep in mind that every analogy, when pressed too far, becomes misleading and distorts the concept and practice of teaching. Every idea that emerges about the teacher has the potential to create haze as well as sunshine, including those Dewey offers. Among the helpful analogies are those that illuminate the heart of teaching, that make clear secondary nuances of teaching, and that reveal marginal ideas about teaching. In examining every analogy, then, we have the responsibility to distinguish the haze and the sunshine and the heart and the periphery as we seek to understand and practice the art of teaching. Teaching, therefore, remains a distinctive art even though it is similar to many others.

We have hinted at a couple of reasons for examining John Dewey's thoughts about the teacher; for example, he suggests compelling, insightful, and multiple images of the teacher and, thereby, helps us avoid reducing the responsibilities of the teacher to a single and perhaps simplistic analogy. He also is wise enough to know that no one figure of speech, comparison, or literal depiction captures the richness and complexity of teaching. He is worth studying, too, because his analogies and other claims form a pattern for understanding the teacher in the broader context of an educational theory or philosophy of education. This advantage is an important one, for a study of isolated and decontextualized images of the teacher can be misleading. For example, both Richard

---

An Introspective Moment

Which figure of speech regarding the teacher beautifully expresses a major portion of how you view the teacher? What's attractive about the analogy? How might it cause you to focus too much on only one aspect of teaching? Does Dewey mention another figure that appeals to you? If yes, how does it complement or amplify the initial image you selected?

Peters and John Holt speak of the teacher as a guide, but their educational theories are drastically different: The former stresses the importance of getting on the inside of forms of knowledge, and the latter focuses his attention on freeing the student to follow her interests. Of course, it should be clear that we can learn much from Dewey's images of the teacher even if we disagree in important ways with his broader educational approach.

We have selected more than a dozen or so of Dewey's images of the teacher to study in this brief work, that is, the teacher as artist, lover, wise mother, navigator, gardener, pioneer, social servant, engineer, curriculum builder, group leader, composer, wise physician, and community constructor. Hidden in these discussions are other less prominent and sometimes overlapping but compelling images of the teachers, e.g., guide, mediator, director, copartner, helper, starter, mediator, interpreter, organizer, watcher, metalworker, researcher, midwife, usher, salesperson, farmer, and conductor. A more exhaustive study of Dewey reveals a host of other images of the teacher (e.g., citizen, prophet, learner, chef, nurse, participator, judge, critic), embedded in his thought, hidden but sometimes sitting on the surface to be scooped up by the miner of his works.

We begin our study with the teacher as artist. We could have said the artist of pedagogy or the art of teaching, for, as we note in the following, Dewey seems to speak of the teacher *being* an artist as well as being *like* an artist. We selected this starting point for several reasons. First, it is one of Dewey's earliest and latest depictions of the teacher. The continuity and development of this image in his voluminous writings indicate how important the concept is to him. Second, it appears that he speaks of the teacher as an artist in both a figurative and a literal sense. The teacher is *like* an artist and *is* an artist. This frame of reference is, perhaps, unique among great educational thinkers and, once again, suggests the critical place this image has in his thought. Third, the teacher as artist appears to be the chief and overarching image of the teacher from his point of view. That is to say, given Dewey's view of the artist, the other images of the teacher—for example, lover, wise parent, pioneer, and so forth—offer enlarging, enriching insights into this basic idea. These distinctive images broaden our vision of the teacher and help us avoid the attractive abyss of collapsing a panoramic view of the teacher into a single snapshot. Fourth, looking at Dewey's beliefs enables us to enter his important, challenging, and often neglected—at least by educators—book *Art as Experience* (1934; LW 10) in an oblique way.

Art as Experience is not for the casual reader but is a book for the person who wishes to grapple with Dewey's broader implications for the art of teaching, the teacher as artist, and the aesthetics of teaching and learning. If there is time, we recommend reading *Art as Experience* along with this work. You will also find that portions of *Democracy and Education* (1916; MW 9), *Experience and Nature* (1929; LW 1), *How We Think* (revised 1933; LW 8), and *Experience and Education* (1938; LW 13) offer valuable insights into the art of teaching. And so, studying Dewey enables us to situate his views of the teacher in his broader educational theory or philosophy, a framework that is both greatly admired and criticized in educational circles.

This book's chapters are usually divided into the following categories:

1. the chapter title,

2. an opening citation or epigraph by Dewey,

3. the text itself,

4. quotes from Dewey and questions for reflection and discussion,

5. implications of the chapter for the teacher,

6. related readings by Dewey, and

7. endnotes.

In addition, we include three different activities in chapters that we think will enable the reader to better understand the concepts being discussed:

8. creating a snapshot of a teacher by using the ideas discussed,

9. analyzing one's own strengths and challenges by engaging in an introspective moment, and

10. considering reflective questions about the thoughts discussed.

Moreover, we intersperse a series of figures throughout the book to summarize, clarify, and illustrate ideas. Finally, we have created an opportunity for the reader to record some concluding thoughts for the chapter under the heading of "A Summative Exercise." A table (see Table 1.1, The Artistic Teacher) at the end of each chapter provides a convenient way for the reader to record a few highlights regarding the teacher as artist.

Table 1.1 The Artistic Teacher

Chapter	Understandings	Qualities	Activities
1	Bodies of knowledge, personal techniques, and vision of student development	Creative, enthusiastic, and imaginative	Thinks for herself

This organizational pattern is designed to facilitate the interests of different readers, such as the snatch-a-few-words reader, the chapter-a-day reader, the member-of-a-discussion-group reader, the I'm-on-my-summer-break reader, the if-I-have-to-I-will reader, and the supplementary-textbook-assignment reader. You may just wish to scan the initial quotes and related text and ignore the rest. Or, alternatively, you may find that you have both the time and interest to take advantage of all of the material. Ideally, the organization of chapters will facilitate your plans whether they involve skimming, scanning, or studying.

We hope you enjoy Dewey's thinking and that his ideas encourage you to keep refining your own reflective, dynamic picture of the teacher as you develop your equally reflective, dynamic practice as an artist.

IMPLICATIONS FOR THE TEACHER

Before moving to the next chapter, let's stop to think about the opening citation or epigraph. Several ideas strike us as being important. First, Dewey says that it is difficult to always be a creative artist. Thinking that artistic teaching is easy is a mistake if he is correct. Thinking that we can be artistic in each teaching activity is also an error. Even the best of artists have to engage in nonartistic activities and do work that does not meet their standards. Painters and sculptors, for example, discard or destroy many of their efforts. They are disappointed with what they have envisioned or created. Of course, we do not have the luxury of taking back our efforts, but we can start again. So we are not like those artists who can dispose of their efforts but like performers—actors, dancers, musicians—who work with a live audience. But we can keep trying to improve our work and grow as masters of the art of teaching. Our ideals, as artists, always remain high.

A Teacher Snapshot

Recall a former teacher who captures the spirit of what Dewey means by enthusiasm, imagination, technique, and vision. Was she considered a great teacher by students? Were there other teachers who lacked these qualities but were also seen as terrific teachers? If so, what qualities did they have that made them effective? Do your memories support or undermine Dewey's point of view?

Second, Dewey observes that artistic teaching entails enthusiasm, imagination, technique, and vision. We will return to these topics later, but for now it is worth noting that he is saying anyone who consistently lacks any of these four—enthusiasm, imagination, technique, and vision—is jeopardizing her standing among the ranks of pedagogical artists. Tending these qualities, dispositions, and skills, then, is imperative, if he is correct. This thought leads us to a series of questions: What should we do for ourselves when our enthusiasm for teaching is waning? Our imagination is inadequate? Our techniques are sterile and repetitive? Our vision is blurred or fading? How do we help one another when we notice needs in these areas?

Third, there is an implicit implication in Dewey's acknowledgment that teaching is a complex, subtle, and nuanced set of understandings, insights, attitudes, judgments, and activities. What is this implication? If we imagine an hour in the life of a teacher, we obtain a glimpse of the implication. We start the school day by hanging up our coat and hiding our purse in the lower drawer of the desk, trying to eliminate the gremlins that infiltrated the computers overnight, welcoming the university intern, and ensuring that as students arrive, each becomes immediately engaged in learning activities. Next, we locate the missing math manipulatives, answer the intern's questions, get each student's attention as she arrives, listen to announcements over the intercom, assist Hannah in the restroom, ask the intern to request that the secretary call Omar's father about returning the zoo permission form, check on Juan's missing materials, ask Letitia to return to her desk, tell Scott to leave Melanie alone, survey the class to determine if everyone is present, complete necessary forms for the office, organize students into groups, get students' attention as we explain a few prerequisite ideas, initiate a study of a math problem, answer students' questions, move quietly but swiftly among the groups to facilitate their learning, walk over to stand beside Bram, confirm the status and progress of each group, secure the class's attention as a group, discuss the solutions of two of the math groups, frown at Pierre as he grabs Zoe's journal, and help students identify the two different methods that were used to solve the same math problem. Then, we remind the class of the importance of respecting each other, prepare the class for physical education, take Kierra to the hallway and encourage her to begin walking in the direction of the learning resources center, walk the class to the gym for physical education, talk with the intern about her activities for the rest of the day, regroup our thoughts for the return of the class, and welcome the class back from gym. Only four and a half hours to go, if we believe the district manual.

What is the implication we are suggesting? For us, it is that the teacher, if she is an artist, is an educational maestro, a professional who integrates "the activities of a busy classroom or extramural project with the skill of a great orchestral conductor." For the students, there is "a wonderful experience" (LW 11: 544). For the outsider, there is a miracle. Unfortunately, the same early morning hour may be overwhelming to many new teachers, because they need to practice their art for years before they become genuine artists (MW 3: 253–254). They need excellent university preparation and school practica if they are going to survive in these early years and happily thrive later. But they are unlikely to live to tell about their experiences, much less flourish, if they do not have regular interactions with the accomplished orchestral conductors in their schools. Future great conductors should profit much from their studies in universities and conservatories, but they arise and grow with orchestras. Magnificent teachers are the same; they flourish in schools. To think otherwise is, candidly, to fail to think. To fail to plan for continuous professional growth after university is to let down both aspiring and practicing artists. Consequently, it will be useful if we think of ourselves as aspiring orchestral conductors. Or, maybe, it will be helpful to think of ourselves as facilitators of budding orchestral conductors if we are administrators, mentors, or teacher educators.

NOTES

1. The feminine pronoun is used throughout this work to refer to both men and women.

2. See *Exploring the Moral Heart of Teaching: Toward a Teacher's Creed* (Teachers College Press, 2001). Interestingly, Hansen has profited immeasurably from examining the treasures of Dewey's thinking.

TWO

The Teacher as Artist

I believe that the art of thus giving shape to human powers and adapting them to social service, is the supreme art; one calling into service the best of artists; that no insight, sympathy, tact, executive power is too great for such service.

—John Dewey (EW 5: 94)

Who wants to be an artist? Perhaps all of us do at one time or another. Many of us, at least, have fantasized about painting landscapes, strumming guitars, standing center stage as lead singers, acting in plays, sculpting busts of great people, writing mystery novels, or conducting city symphonies. If we are aspiring or practicing teachers, we also dream of and have educational experiences that are aesthetically fulfilling, emotionally exquisite, intellectually delicious, and personally rewarding. Sometimes these experiences are sprinkled like glowing gems throughout the days, weeks, months, and years. Occasionally, they burst forth as sparkling diamonds that are overwhelming to everyone involved. Often, they are priceless moments or

Authors' Note: References to works by John Dewey are from the collection of his works published by Southern Illinois University Press: *The Early Works of John Dewey, 1882–1898*; *The Middle Works of John Dewey, 1899–1924*; and *The Later Works of John Dewey, 1925–1953*. References to these works are abbreviated as EW, MW, and LW, where, for example, EW 5: 94 indicates that the material cited or idea noted is in *The Early Works*, Volume 5, page 94.

products of small group, semiprivate, and individual activities. Unknowingly, we may have had feelings that are similar to those of an exceptional artist who revels in the pleasure of having been a part of phenomenal artistic moment and aesthetic experience. We know, too, that our students have had experiences that have helped make them beautifully different, more insightful, reflective, and whole.

Who wants to be an artist? Ideally, all of us do if we are or want to be teachers, for each of us has artistic abilities and potentialities in the realm of teaching, according to Dewey. Thus, the question is not whether we have artistic abilities, but whether we will support, cultivate, polish, and use them.

But we all have our own highly personal images of what the artist is like, how she conceives her role, prepares for her work, and performs her duties. These differences are, in part, the result of the various images the term *artist* suggests, for example, musician, sculptor, painter, glassblower, conductor, and actress. Our images of the artist also differ at times because of our teaching specialities (e.g., mathematics, music, history, biology) and the students (e.g., preschoolers, preteenagers, teenagers) we teach. Similarly, our cultures, contexts, and

> **A Teacher Snapshot**
>
> Think of an experience you have had or observed when a teacher guided a student or a group to stop and think—reconsider—their desires or ideas. Was she successful? Why do you think she was or was not?

interests influence the way we think about the artist. Plus, our personalities and imaginations are reflected in our images of what it takes to soar as an educational artist. The riches of life, however they are labeled, influence our creative insights into these questions.

Before we pursue our own thinking about the artist, let's look at Dewey's view for a moment.[1] As we can tell by the above quotation, as he writes "My Pedagogic Creed" (1897) Dewey thinks of the teacher as a person who helps give shape to and adapts the abilities of children and youth. Years later in *Experience and Education*, he continues to express the same thoughts, arguing that the teacher needs to take the existing impulses and desires of students and assist in the remaking of them, so that these inclinations and interests become transformed into intelligently conceived and planned purposes. The process of transformation involves the teacher and student cooperating—much like a director and actor—as the student becomes more intellectually capable, personally independent, and socially responsible. Among other things, Dewey claims that the transformation involves the artist knowing when and how to get the student to stop and consider the consequences of thinking, feeling, and behaving in certain ways. To get students to stop and think, the full range of the teacher's artistic abilities will need to be developed and used.

Who wants to be an artist? Ideally, those people who are sensitive to shaping the whole student in ethically justifiable ways.

We can also tell from Dewey's comment that he thinks teaching isn't a job for those who aren't insightful, sympathetic, and tactful. Nor is teaching for those who lack the ability to execute or carry out their responsibilities. Moreover, teaching is not for those who have very limited abilities. Those who become the best artists need natural and highly developed abilities, because they are participating in the supreme art. The highest art demands nothing less than a liberally educated teacher who uses her knowledge, experience, and abilities to keep growing in her understanding of professional knowledge, pedagogical practice, student development, and educational means. Only by growing in these areas can we both be and remain inventive artists.

Who wants to be an artist? Ideally, those of us who know the importance of becoming liberally educated, highly competent, deeply interested, and keenly perceptive professionals.

Another idea seems worth mentioning, too. Dewey's particular interpretation of education is that it is vitally related to adapting human abilities for social service. He does not think students should learn to read, write, calculate, paint, sculpt, act, and think simply so they can get into good universities and be offered high-paying jobs after graduation. Students need to develop a view of life that helps them get beyond personal interests and consider the interests of others, including their schools, communities, nation, and world. Their developed abilities, perceptions, and sensitivities should be adapted to meet the needs of society, including promoting a culture that takes into consideration the importance of people living democratically, which means much more than just voting for political candidates and obeying the laws of a region. Doing chemistry, history, biology, art, physics, music, and psychology are socially important activities and should be learned with more than individual development and career ambitions in mind. For Dewey, each child and youth is a social and ethical being—not an isolated or narcissistic intellect—who needs to learn to use what she learns for the well-being of others. The student, as a result, is much more than a son or daughter. Ultimately, because she is a social being and a member of society, she has responsibilities for its development, socially, politically, economically, and ethically. Education for leadership, therefore, is an important aim of the school, and this aim is inclusive; that is, it is not limited to the few students who usually get involved in student government, academic clubs, and honor societies (EW 5: 57–59).

Who wants to be an artist? Ideally, it is people who have a vision of a democratic society that needs, encourages, and enjoys the contributions of everyone.

As we stated earlier, we think that Dewey's overarching image of the teacher is that of artist. Consequently, the complementary images presented hereinafter are either explicitly or implicitly loaded with artistic suggestions. Sometimes we note these suggestions; other times we do not. Whatever our response, we think Dewey hopes that the teacher images discussed throughout this work will promote artistic insight for teachers and, thereby, aesthetic experiences for them and their students.

QUOTES AND QUESTIONS

As we think about art and the teacher, several dimensions of art may occur to us. For example, we can think of art as an activity, the art of teaching. Dewey comments in *Art as Experience* on this:

> Art denotes a process of doing or making. This is as true of fine as of technological art. Art involves molding of clay, chipping of marble, casting of bronze, laying on of pigments, construction of buildings, singing of songs, playing of instruments, enacting roles on the stage, and going through rhythmic movements in the dance. (LW 10: 53)

He adds:

> The doing or making is artistic when the perceived result is of such a nature that *its* qualities *as perceived* have controlled the question of production. The act of producing that is directed by intent to produce something that is enjoyed in the immediate experience has qualities that a spontaneous or uncontrolled activity does not have. The artist embodies in himself the attitude of the perceiver while he works. (LW 10: 55)

The quality of art as an activity includes both "the manner and content of doing," or how the artist does her work and the content that is intrinsic to the doing of her work. Dewey thus implies that the methods and outcomes of teaching cannot be separated from the teacher's aims. As the teacher's method of teaching is controlled by her aims, she produces outcomes that are artistically and aesthetically satisfying. But the content that is intrinsically a part of one's method—such as respect for students, appreciation of democratic values, and enthusiasm for one's art—is also taught indirectly (LW 10: 218).

The first of our quotes in this section suggests an important question: Given that teaching is—or at least is similar to—an art, what kinds of activities clarify its nature? Dewey uses the terms *shaping, enacting, adapting, singing,* and *molding* to capture some of the artistic activities of the teacher. What terms would you use to describe the activities of the teacher as artist? What terms would you want to avoid? Are there any limits that should be placed on the kinds of activities that may be considered artistic? Why? In what ways is teaching *not* like many other artistic endeavors, for example, molding clay or chipping marble? How do you think these activities are similar to teaching?

The second quote from Dewey suggests some ideas that may or may not apply to the artistic teacher. Does the intent of the teacher, for instance, need to control the perceived result? Can it? Should immediate educative experiences always be characterized by enjoyment? In what ways, if at all, should the teacher embody the attitude of the student as she works? By the way, what is the attitude of the student? How would such an attitude help the teacher? The student? In what ways can the comparisons between the teacher and other artists be misleading?

IMPLICATIONS FOR THE TEACHER

What do Dewey's ideas suggest about the teacher being a member of a guild or family of artists? Several ideas provide hints about artistic teaching. First, he puts forward the notion that artists are characterized by having well-developed "insight, sympathy, tact, executive power[s]" (EW 5: 94). Although he does not give us sufficient information to interpret some of these concepts, we can still ask ourselves some questions:

A Reflective Opportunity

If a teacher lacks sympathy or tact, how do you think this will affect her teaching? If a friend asks you to offer her advice on developing insight into students, are you helping her become a better artist? Is there anything a person can do to nurture these qualities?

In what realms do teachers most need insight? Sympathy? Tact? Executive powers? Slow down a minute to consider a question: What do our answers to these questions tell us about the teacher as artist? About ourselves?

Second, Dewey informs us that pedagogical artists are concerned with shaping and adapting human powers. Embedded in this claim are several ethical considerations: Teachers as artists are engaged in activities that are designed to improve both students and society. His proposal is that artists are concerned with enabling students to accomplish what they were previously incapable of doing and doing such for themselves and others. Indirectly, he is suggesting that teaching and artistry are permeated with value questions. For example, how should a teacher, school, and district go about deciding how and in what ways they will seek to improve students in the area of social behavior? How would Dewey answer the question?

Third, art, like teaching, is, in part, an activity. The activity of teaching may be artistic if it meets certain conditions, for process per se is not necessarily an art. An activity is artistic when the perceived qualities of the outcome have controlled the process of creation too. That is to say, we are artistic when we recognize in our methods of teaching the goals we pursued and the results we achieved. We may, then, ask: What qualities do we wish to see in students, and are we using—and personifying—these same qualities in the creative process? Do we employ imagination as we nurture it? Are we reflective as we cultivate reflection? How do we exhibit caring as we foster the disposition and its behavioral manifestations? When we are developing democratic attitudes and inclinations, are we democratic ourselves? Are our pedagogical activities characterized by the qualities of educated people as we seek to facilitate their growth? Also, do we enjoy the activities that we want our students to enjoy?

We may think that nearly any profession or type of work could be seen through these three windows:

1. an insightful, sympathetic, tactful execution of responsibilities;

2. a shaping of personal powers for individual and social use; and

3. an enjoyable activity that is characterized by what one wishes to accomplish.

If so, are people who pursue these activities artists too? Dewey's answer is that the artistic and aesthetic are—or at least can be—in nearly every activity and experience, and that we need to reclaim the ordinary aspects of life and work (LW 10: 18). But both the process and product of these activities must be life encouraging, enabling, enhancing, and enriching if they are genuinely artistic (LW 10: 20; LW 1: 271). Does it lessen the value of the artist if nearly any activity can call forth the qualities and attitudes of the artist? Not if we agree with Dewey's vantage point. Nor if we value everyday life and its activities and believe it and they need to be imbued with the artistic and aesthetic spirit. Nor if we realize that genuine art in any domain is a rare find and important need in any culture. The barren educational cultures of many schools may be most needy, for they are artistically and aesthetically starved. Given Dewey's philosophy, it explains why he can refer to ethics (MW 3: 42), habits (MW 14: 14–15, 47–48), medicine (LW 3: 26), science (LW 1: 287), and philosophy (LW 16: 369) as art and to the arts of teaching, questioning, guiding (LW 8: 331–332), thinking (LW 1: 287), and instructing (MW 9: 164).

Art is rare even if found in everyday activities and experiences. It involves a challenging set of activities, and this means that we have to develop our insight, sympathy, tact, and executive powers. Likewise, it indicates that we must refine our own shaping skills and other abilities if we want to work artistically with students. Furthermore, we often need to create more and better opportunities for students to grow in and contribute to their classes, schools, and communities, for they are both participants in and recipients of our performing art.

A SUMMATIVE EXERCISE

Chapter 2   The Teacher as Artist

Understandings	Qualities	Activities

READINGS

"Experience, Nature and Art," in *Experience and Nature* (LW 1: 266–294).
"The Live Creature," in *Art as Experience* (LW 10: 9–25).
"The Recitation and the Training of Thought," in *How We Think: A Restatement of the Relation of Reflective Thinking to the Educative Process* (LW 8: 326–341).

NOTE

1. The details of Dewey's artistic and aesthetic thought are beyond the scope of this brief work. For more insight into his artistic and aesthetic thinking, see his *Art as Experience* and Philip Jackson's *John Dewey and the Lessons of Art* (Yale University Press, 1998). Conversely, the aspects of Dewey's artistic and aesthetic thinking that are contextually critical are integrated in the text.

THREE

The Teacher
as Lover

A natural love of contact with the young . . . a natural love of communicating knowledge . . . a love of knowledge . . . [a] love of arousing in others the same intellectual interests and enthusiasms . . . an unusual love . . . [of] some one subject . . . [a] love of learning . . . [characterize the successful teacher].

—John Dewey (LW 13: 344–345)

The teacher as lover? A weird idea, isn't it? If it is for us, it isn't for Dewey.

He envisions a teacher who is a lover of learning, knowledge, a particular subject, interacting with students, communicating knowledge, and arousing students' intellectual curiosity. And more. But let's begin with these six loves and, during the voyage, add two others: a love of others and a love of thinking.

In "To Those Who Aspire to the Profession of Teaching" (1938), Dewey states that a prospective teacher should seriously consider a number of matters before deciding on whether to enter teaching. Interestingly, he does not make

---

Authors' Note: References to works by John Dewey are from the collection of his works published by Southern Illinois University Press: *The Early Works of John Dewey, 1882–1898*; *The Middle Works of John Dewey, 1899–1924*; and *The Later Works of John Dewey, 1925–1953*. References to these works are abbreviated as EW, MW, and LW, where, for example, EW 5: 94 indicates that the material cited or idea noted is in *The Early Works*, Volume 5, page 94.

an indiscriminate appeal to people to get them to enter the profession. Nor does he make an appeal to a narrow band of intellectually talented prospects. His view of the artistic teacher is a very sophisticated one, one that reaches beyond the realms of the expected. He discusses his views under three general headings: the opportunities, the demands, and the difficulties of the profession. Although the three realms overlap, the second is particularly important in understanding his view of the qualities that enable a teacher to be both successful and artistic (LW 13: 342).

He begins by discussing the prospective teacher's health and moves to her emotional fitness. Teaching is taxing, emotionally and physically, and, to be sure, there are those who should not be allowed to work with children and youth. But in addition, he advises those who are especially anxious and nervous not to pursue teaching, because he thinks they will probably have a negative effect on the children they teach. In essence, he believes that the anxiety and apprehensiveness of a person will contribute to her being an unhappy and ineffective educator. In context, he argues for the first kind of love that aspiring teachers should have, and that highly anxious and apprehensive people may not have: a love of being involved with children or youth. Dewey believes that when a teacher does not have this love, students will easily detect that she does not enjoy being with them. Students easily identify, he says, the teachers who work out of obligation, not out of interest in them (LW 13: 344). A love of contact with students is also crucially important in the teacher's coming to have an extensive understanding of them and, thereby, diagnosing their educational needs, which, according to Dewey in *Democracy and Education*, is a basis for the teacher being able to artistically teach each student (MW 9: 177). Put candidly, he says two things about the art of teaching: that insight into students and the ability to diagnose their needs are prerequisites to being an artistic teacher. An in-depth, personal, and growing knowledge of each student, therefore, is an imperative for the artist of pedagogy.

Dewey's exact words deserve attention. Although he believes that teachers should love students themselves, he does not specifically say so in this instance. In the quotation, Dewey says teachers should love *contact with* the young. This love obviously involves developing a set of positive relationships, including an enjoyment of interacting with students (LW 13: 343). The teacher, it appears, is to love contact with students but to avoid a parental or emotional attachment that may prejudice her professional judgment (LW 13: 343). Neither pedagogical expertise nor content mastery, Dewey adds, can overcome a lack of this kind of love. Technical facility and knowledge of subject matter alone are inadequate. Consequently, only those who have and use the ability to stay young and sympathize with children or adolescents should remain teachers very long. Or, to revise the statement slightly, only those who desire to interact with students should be teachers (LW 13: 344). Those who lack these qualities should not even consider teaching as a career. Enjoying contact with children, staying young at heart, and retaining sympathy for the young, then, reach into the core of what

> **A Reflective Opportunity**
> ---
> Why do you think it is difficult for some teachers to love or respect a student? Can a person learn to love or respect students who are genuinely unlikable? If your answer is yes, what can a person do to facilitate change?

Dewey means by this type of love of the successful teacher. Even so, simply loving to be with children or youth does not guarantee that a person will be an effective teacher. Once again, much more is required. The person who enjoys being with children or adolescents should certainly nourish this interest but also look beyond it to other important qualifications.

One of these qualifications is a second kind of love, one that Dewey discusses in his book *Psychology* (1887–1891). There he writes of parental, filial, and religious loves, describing them as an interest in others' well-being (EW 2: 249, 293–294). Later, he amplifies the idea of familial love and, by extension, community-wide and universal love. He says that this kind of love—today we might call this kind of love respect for others—is an intentional choice to seek another's good and, when applied to society, includes promoting the common good (MW 5: 518). The loving teacher seeks the individual good of every student as well as the common good of students and society. This love of others seems foundational to Dewey's social, political, moral, and pedagogical thought and is deemed essential for the teacher who is constantly moving in and among school and external communities. Such love, of course, demands the guidance of reflective thinking if it is to be profitably applied. When reflection is used in the interest of individuals and society, it provides an important point of reference, suggesting thoughts often not found in the thinking of other, more process-oriented advocates of democratic schools. The teacher who works in a Deweyan democratic school loves colleagues and students in the sense that she intentionally pursues their good. Being interested in the welfare of others, she can more readily see the need to adapt the abilities of students for the good of society. The absence of this kind of love results in the marginalization of individuals and groups in school and undermines the artistic interests of the teacher.

Immediately after discussing a love of contact with students, Dewey mentions two other loves required for pedagogical success: a love of knowledge and a love of communicating it (LW 13: 344–345). Although both kinds of love are necessary for being a successful, artistic teacher, again neither by itself nor both combined is sufficient for the teacher Dewey visualizes. Contrary to what many school critics today appear to believe, he thinks that the third kind of love, a passion for knowledge, alone does not make a person a successful teacher, just as he believes that the fourth love of communicating is by itself an insufficient quality. A love of knowledge in general assists the teacher as she understands, interprets, and explains the interconnectedness of fields of inquiry and, thereby, life. But the love of knowledge—also called a "love of truth for truth's sake"—suggests an enjoyment of playing with ideas that teachers should pass on to their students (MW 7: 322). A love of communicating, then, must be attached to sharing something, namely knowledge, not just unwarranted personal opinion. Note that Dewey is in favor of the teacher's communicating ideas, information, and knowledge, which is a part of her responsibility to create an environment that stimulates learning. The teacher has a responsibility to learn, be passionate about what she knows, and share some of what she loves with students.

At this stage, we need to examine further his idea of creating a learning environment. Four points deserve attention. First, it is crucial to understand that the teacher's love and pursuit of knowledge is, in part, an ongoing process of self-creation. Second, this process of personal creation— the teacher's creating herself by continuing to grow—is an intrinsic part of the activity of fashioning a learning environment for students. That is, the teacher is actively preparing a significant aspect of the learning environment—herself—when she learns more about students, teaching, learning, community, and subject matter. Third, creating a broader learning environment does not shift weight away from the teacher's responsibility to communicate knowledge. As a result, Dewey argues that teachers should be so well prepared in their subjects that their knowledge richly overflows (LW 8: 338). Finally, this knowledge, combined with matured experience, enables the teacher to be the leader in the classroom, a topic that we will return to later (LW 8: 337).

We also need to stop briefly to examine what Dewey means by natural love and the natural teacher. He elaborates on the notion of a natural love for communicating by saying that the person who is a natural teacher does not view learning as complete without the opportunity to share what has been learned. The natural-born teacher, Dewey declares, uses knowledge and her enthusiasm for it to plant a spark and eventually ignite the flames of learning and thinking in others (LW 13: 345). So, it seems that Dewey believes that a natural-born teacher is a person who has particular gifts or inclinations that give her a decided edge in becoming a great teacher (LW 13: 345). These gifts or inclinations include a definite and lively interest in the thinking and feelings of children or youth (LW 13: 345) and a bent toward enthusiastically sharing with them what she knows. But the natural-born teacher can still profit greatly by having these gifts nurtured in a teacher preparation program, and other educators can benefit by having the gifted teacher's abilities, attitudes, and qualities studied (LW 5: 4–5).

Dewey's fifth love is implicit in our previous discussion, a love of stimulating interest in the subjects for which she has great interest and enthusiasm (LW 13: 345). This love seems to be firmly joined with the love of communicating knowledge and is at least one desired outcome of that communication. Here it is easy to see how arousing students' interest in living and stirring ideas is tied to behavioral change and moral development. Without the love of stimulating others' interest in a subject or issue, it is difficult to think that moral education—or any other kind of education—can be successful (MW 4: 267). This love is critical, in part, because its enthusiasm is so

> ### An Introspective Moment
>
> If you do not have a burning passion for anything you teach or plan to teach, should you reconsider your career plans? Are there other options? What made you draw this conclusion?

powerful, surpassing even the force of methodological expertise: "A genuine enthusiasm is an attitude that operates as an intellectual force. A teacher who arouses such an enthusiasm in his pupils has done something that no amount of formalized method, no matter how correct, can accomplish" (LW 8: 137).

A sixth love, alluded to previously, is what Dewey identifies as an extraordinary love for one field of study (LW 13: 345). This love for and aptitude in one particular subject appears to overlap with the "love of knowledge itself." Yet Dewey qualifies his statement in important ways. First, the love is an unusual, not ordinary, passion. Second, it is for one subject, not for knowledge in general. These two ideas suggest that the teacher—and for Dewey this applies to all kindergarten through 12th-grade teachers[1]—needs a particularly strong love for at least one of the subjects she teaches. Third, Dewey clarifies that a love of knowledge in general and a strong love of one field is not enough: Aptitude in the subject is also required. But aptitude without love is also undesirable: A person who is uncommitted to intellectual growth and slithers along the bottom academically is not the kind of person Dewey wants teaching. Why is Dewey so firm on this point? In part, it is because he wants students to have capable teachers who are passionate about their fields of expertise. But he also wants them to have teachers who demonstrate the ability to think critically and imaginatively in these fields. He wants students to catch the passion and learn to think like the teacher. That is to say, he wants students who are passionate about knowledge and thinking for themselves.

This love of a subject illuminates why Dewey subscribes to a seventh love of the successful teacher: a contagious love of learning (LW 13: 345). At first glance, this love may seem to be identical with a love of stirring intellectual interests in others, but Dewey may intend subtle differences. First, the intentional love of arousing a student's intellectual interest and enthusiasm may be different from unconsciously spreading a contagion for learning. Second, arousing in a student the same intellectual interests may be different from passing on a contagious love of learning in general or a love of learning that leads into different intellectual interests. Third, although akin to a love for knowledge, a love of learning is manifestly dynamic and not satisfied with loving that which has already been acquired. In any event, the complementary relationship of intentionally arousing love of intellectual matters in students and unconsciously spreading a love of learning to them suggests the multiple ways Dewey wishes to nurture an excitement for and about educative activities.

In *The Quest for Certainty*, Dewey (LW 4: 182) argues for yet another love, an eighth one that applies to the successful teacher: a love of thinking that leads to an interest in solving problems (LW 4: 182). This love, in certain respects, encapsulates the other loves and may explain the professional enthusiasm and dedication of excellent teachers and the spirit of openness and inquiry that characterizes their classrooms. Likewise, it may help explain why there is, on the part of some, a growing interest in preparing educators and students to think critically and be open minded in examining intellectual issues.

Table 3.1 The Loves of a Successful Teacher

Type	Relevance to Teaching
Others	Respects each student regardless of background
Contact with the young	Enjoys being and working with students
Learning	Keeps growing as a person and professional
Knowledge	Enjoys distinguishing between warranted conclusions and unfounded opinions
A subject	Manifests a depth of understanding and thinking
Communicating knowledge	Takes pleasure in articulating what she understands
Arousing intellectual interests	Values the opportunity to stimulate curiosity
Thinking	Prizes evaluative and reflective thinking

A love of thinking is also significant for another reason, one central to this book. Dewey specifies that thinking—because it is an activity or entails a set of activities—may be seen as an art (LW 8: 182). The teacher's process of thinking about educational and classroom challenges should be done in an artistic fashion—or in a way that draws on the best experiences, observations, data, critiques, and experimentation available. As he implies in *Democracy and Education*, the teacher whose thinking is judiciously guided toward carefully selected ends engages in one aspect of the art of teaching, namely the art of thinking (MW 9: 177). Having an engaged, thinking, artistic teacher is one of the greatest gifts that a student can receive, Dewey believes. He identifies this love with a "love of inquiry into the puzzling and unknown" and with the "development of curiosity, suggestion, and habits of exploring and testing, which increases sensitiveness to questions" (LW 8: 156).

These eight loves—of others, contact with the young, learning, knowledge, one subject, communicating knowledge, arousing intellectual interests, and thinking—are obviously interwoven and may reflect what we often call a love of teaching. Table 3.1 summarizes these loves and suggests one way each is relevant to teaching. These loves also serve two immediate purposes. First, they make central Dewey's volitional, rational, and communitarian conceptions of love—love as a thoughtful concern for promoting the individual and common good or the good of others. We might also talk here of an affective love or ethic of care that is rooted in his thought. A volitional love or equal respect of students and a passionate love for interacting with students, communicating knowledge to them, and arousing their intellectual curiosity seem to fit nicely with the idea that we should care for their well-being as people. Second, they address two common misconceptions about Dewey: (1) that he advocates a sentimental love of children that encourages teachers to allow students to follow their interests wherever they take them and (2) that he overemphasizes independent learning by students to the exclusion of valuing content and the involvement of teachers in the class-room. People who have drawn these latter two conclusions have not enjoyed the opportunity of reading Dewey's works.

QUOTES AND QUESTIONS

In Chapter 2, we discussed briefly art as an activity. So, observing that the teacher as lover is involved in numerous activities that may be done artistically is no minor discovery. The activities of communicating, learning, discovering, and arousing interest, to mention just a few, can all be pursued artistically. But there are other sides of art, including the product that we noted in passing. An exploration of the idea of art as a product is now in order. To begin, we should admit that many people may not particularly like the idea of the student being viewed as a product, artistic or not. This is understandable because people differ in kind from other objects of art—for example, paintings, compositions, plays, statues, buildings, and poetry—in that we are living creatures who think and choose for ourselves. This precise point is noted by Dewey in "The Classroom Teacher" (1924) when he declares:

> When we come to dealing with living things, especially living characters that vary as human individuals do, and attempt to modify their individual dispo-sitions, develop their individual powers, counteract their individual interests, we have to deal with them in an artistic way, a way which requires sympathy and interest to make all of the needed adjustments to the particular emergen-cies of the act. The more mechanical a thing is, the more we can manage it; the more vital it is, the more we have to use our observation and interest in order to adjust ourselves properly to it. It is not easy, in other words, to main-tain a truly artistic standard, which is, of course, the real business of the teacher. (MW 15: 180)

He complements this thought in "Philosophies of Freedom" (1928) by saying:

A genuine energetic interest in the cause of human freedom will manifest itself in a jealous and unremitting care for the influence of social institutions upon the attitudes of curiosity, inquiry, weighing and testing evidence. I shall begin to believe that we care more for freedom than we do for imposing our own beliefs upon others in order to subject them to our will, when I see that the main purpose of our schools and other institutions is to develop powers of unremitting and discriminating observation and judgment. (LW 3: 113)

Here we see Dewey's notion of love of or respect for others. Love for others requires, among other things, a concern for their freedom, the development of their abilities including the ability to think, and the building of schools that promote all three—loving others, nurturing freedom, and encouraging reflection. If we genuinely love or respect students, then, we will not exploit or manipulate them, either for personal or ideological ends. Love will not let us do that—or at least, if it is sufficiently strong it will not allow us to habitually use students as we would objects or financial resources. We

> **A Teacher Snapshot**
>
> In a sense, may the act of thinking also be an art product? Can you describe a teacher or colleague who both exemplifies and cultivates this product?

cannot live our lives through students if we genuinely respect them. A passionate love, too, would seem to keep us from trying to make our students replicas of us: "Craftsmanship to be artistic in the final sense must be 'loving'; it must care deeply for the subject matter upon which skill is exercised" (LW 10: 54).

These thoughts may be seen as placing contradictory and unrealistic expectations on the teacher. Can a teacher really be all that Dewey suggests? Is it correct, for instance, to say that a teacher who lacks love for a specific subject matter cannot be educationally artistic? What does this imply about early childhood and elementary teachers who are required to teach several subjects? Are there down-to-earth points of comparisons between artists who work with material objects and artists who work primarily with humans? Are there dangers in the loves, the passions that Dewey encourages or, rather, expects of the teacher?

Several other questions ask for attention: Are there other loves that you think Dewey should discuss? How might his ideas about the eight loves inform the selection of aspiring teachers? In what ways, if any, should the ongoing development of seasoned professionals be influenced by these loves? What are the implications of these loves for multicultural education and the ethical development of students? How do we avoid parental love for our students and at the same time care deeply for them? Indeed, should we avoid a parent-type love for our students?

IMPLICATIONS FOR THE TEACHER

In Chapter 2, we saw that Dewey's thought about the art of teaching and the teacher as artist covers a number of elements, including the ideas that art is a demanding activity and is based on our nurturing our insight, sympathy, tact, executive powers, and shaping skills as well as ensuring that the qualities we seek to develop in our students characterize the educational process itself. Now he tells us more but, in a sense, takes us back to Chapter 1, where we saw his emphasis on enthusiasm being a quality of the creative artist. Being an enthusiastic, even passionate, lover of learning, knowledge, a particular subject, interacting with students, communicating knowledge to them, and arousing their intellectual curiosity ties together his thinking and fits marvelously with the idea of being a creative teacher. If we are artists in classrooms or, alternatively, successful teachers, we need to love being with children, a love that leads to learning about each student so that we can artistically personalize our teaching. Moreover, we need to refine our thinking abilities so that we become intellectual artists and practice and encourage the art of thinking with our students. Plus, there is the implication that our passion for the development of students as products of our educational art is not inconsistent with our respect for them as people who need the freedom to think for and, thereby, to create themselves. Teachers, too, are creators and become co-creators with students but do not impose themselves on those in their care. Here we seem to have a creation paradox: We help create a person who also helps to create us—and a person who goes far beyond our contributions as she intelligently selects her own values and learns to think for herself. Students, then, ultimately but not necessarily immediately have the final say, in that their interests and growth determine what they will feel, think, believe, choose, and become in an artist's classroom. Their freedom— like that of the teacher—is both enhanced and limited by the ethics of a democratically responsible classroom and school.

A SUMMATIVE EXERCISE

Chapter 3 The Teacher as Lover

Understandings	*Qualities*	*Activities*

READINGS

"Philosophies of Freedom," (LW 3: 92–114).
"To Those Who Aspire to the Profession of Teaching," (LW 13: 342–346).
"What Is the Matter with Teaching?", (LW 2: 116–123).

NOTE

1. In Dewey's day, preschool—and often kindergarten—was rare and not a widely accepted idea. It would be consistent with his overall thought to suggest that preschool teachers need this sixth love, too. In fact, it appears safe to say that all teachers should be expected to have a love for a particular subject, even when they teach several different subjects as early and elementary educators often do. Dewey wants children of all ages to learn with teachers who have a passion for and aptitude in a particular field of inquiry or creativity. Their passion and thinking are means of spreading the former and fostering the latter: How can a teacher who shows no sign of caring for a subject communicate interest and enthusiasm for it to others, or even motivate students except by coercion?

FOUR

The Teacher as Wise Mother

The wise mother takes account of the needs of the infant but not in a way which dispenses with her own responsibility for regulating the objective conditions under which the needs are satisfied. And if she is a wise mother in this respect, she draws upon past experiences of experts as well as her own for the insight that these shed upon what experiences are in general most conducive to the normal development of infants.

—John Dewey (LW 13: 23–24)

How often do we think of the home, parents, or caregivers as models of positive educational activities? Not very often is our guess, not even as often as we might first suppose. We are probably influenced by the fact that many homes—from numerous backgrounds—are challenges and difficulties for schools and teachers more often than they are complementary educational agents. But we all know, too, of many parents and homes that are extremely

Authors' Note: References to works by John Dewey are from the collection of his works published by Southern Illinois University Press: *The Early Works of John Dewey, 1882–1898*; *The Middle Works of John Dewey, 1899–1924*; and *The Later Works of John Dewey, 1925–1953*. References to these works are abbreviated as EW, MW, and LW, where, for example, EW 5: 94 indicates that the material cited or idea noted is in *The Early Works*, Volume 5, page 94.

supportive and provide terrific learning environments. If only we could, we might occasionally wish to clone these caregivers and homes if it wouldn't destroy individuality and freedom and artistry. So would Dewey, and he would like to begin by transporting from these desirable homes characteristics and qualities that are relevant to teaching and learning in schools. Of course, Dewey recognizes that there are degrees of providing healthy home environments. No home is completely devoid of positive qualities; neither is any home a totally positive environment.

Dewey's vantage point, then, is from the slant of parents and homes that provide largely constructive settings. He enjoys comparing the teacher to these parents, especially to a wise mother or father. His interest stems as much from the insights he thinks can be had from properly understanding ordinary experiences as from his admiration of parents and teachers. He sees the home as a model learning environment for the school not so much to emulate—because schools are not homes—as to learn from. He thinks we have much to learn about teaching and learning from a home that has wise parents. Learning in homes with wise parents is deemed admirable because they are places where natural—in contrast with contrived or artificial—means of learning are used, where participation is a key factor of learning, where feedback takes place on a regular basis, and where guidance is given by at least several people (adults and children) who understand and are sensitive to the interests and needs of family members. Homes are also places where parents and siblings develop skills, ideas, and abilities that are relevant to everyday life. His book *The School and Society* (revised 1915) tells us how the home cultivates and connects several prized undertakings and values, such as participating in everyday household tasks, developing desirable work habits, increasing one's respect for the rights and ideas of others, appreciating the interests of others, learning to subordinate one's interests periodically to group concerns, and gaining personally pertinent information:

> We find the child learning through the social converse and constitution of the family. There are certain points of interest and value to him in the conversation carried on: statements are made, inquiries arise, topics are discussed, and the child continually learns. He states his experiences; his misconceptions are corrected. Again the child participates in the household occupations, and thereby gets habits of industry, order, and regard for the rights and ideas of others, and the fundamental habit of subordinating his activities to the general interest of the household. Participation in these household tasks becomes an opportunity for gaining knowledge. (MW 1: 23–24)

Partially hidden in Dewey's statement, we find not only some of his values but also insight into family pedagogy and, potentially, school pedagogy: participating in ordinary activities, talking about experiences, raising questions, discussing topics of interest, engaging in conversations, and receiving feedback on misconceptions. So, Dewey's interest in the healthy family comes from both a values and pedagogical perspective. Obliquely, he indicates that he wants values and habits developed in homes and schools that will contribute to a healthy democratic society.

> **An Introspective Moment**
>
> Have you ever felt that you were a member of a genuine community? A learning community? What characteristics did the group have? How would you describe a classroom—or, better, social group—that Dewey has in mind?

Dewey is trying to tell us why and how a home can be so powerful and, indirectly, suggest that the school can be similarly influential if it is a community, not just a place where disconnected bodies, minds, and hearts are rounded up five days a week. In some schools, we may not be this successful: Far too often, just the bodies are corralled, and the minds and hearts are out on the open range. But we know schools that are often very effective and many others that can be much better than they are. Dewey nudges us even further on the matter. He particularly notes, in *Reconstruction in Philosophy* (1920), how family life is involved in the selection of experiences, the development of language, the acquisition of facts, the interpretation of facts and experiences, the cultivation of beliefs, the formation of perceptions, and the initiation of expeditions or inquiries. His upper-middle-class outlook shows, but his fundamental concepts and sociological framework are informative:

> Mother and nurse, father and older children, determine experiences the child shall have; they constantly instruct him as to the meaning of what he does and undergoes. The conceptions that are socially current and important become the child's principles of interpretation and estimation long before he attains to personal and deliberate control of conduct. Things come to him clothed in language, not in physical nakedness, and this garb of communication makes him a sharer in the beliefs of those about him. These beliefs coming to him as so many facts form his mind; they furnish the centers about which his own personal expeditions and perceptions are ordered. (MW 12: 132)

No wonder, given this image of the home, Dewey values it as a model of learning, engagement, and development and encourages us to make our schools similar. When the school and classroom, like the family, are social groups and not merely instructional settings, their power is exponentially extended. The more we engage the whole school and the full resources of each classroom in the processes of teaching and learning, the easier, more exciting, and successful the experiences will be.

But aren't we off the subject? Isn't our subject the wise parent or, if we pay attention to the initial quote, the wise mother? Haven't we been talking about the home as an educational environment instead? Yes, our subject is the wise mother or parent, and we have been discussing the home as an educational model. Are they unrelated, however? We think not, for the wise mother and father—or other caregivers—create a healthy environment for learning in their home. Older children, when they are similarly prepared, help do the same. Nourishing a healthy, educative setting is a critical

> **A Reflective Opportunity**
>
> How can we know when an experience or a research study is worth acting on or sharing with other teachers? Would group reflection and judgment be useful?

responsibility. Fortunately, part of a constructive environment is natural, a given when family members are growing as individuals and a group. But much of the environment is created by reflective thinking and making shrewd choices. How does the parent or teacher or older child go about such thinking and environmental responsibilities? Let's focus on the mother as we answer these questions, because Dewey does.

Our chapter title and initial quote from *Experience and Education* (LW 13: 23–24) implies a general answer to this question: The mother is manifestly wise. She is a reflective and prudent person, and she is a model for the teacher who needs to think and make judgments as she addresses the needs of each student. As the wise parent does not forget the reality of the world around her child and simply allow the child's personal inclinations to determine what is learned, so the wise teacher does not subordinate the external or objective environment of the school (e.g., materials, textbooks, computers, microscopes, library) to the internal or subjective needs of the student (e.g., impulses, desires, purposes). Her thinking and decision making are more reflective, complicated, and challenging as she keeps in mind her responsibilities as a well-educated professional educator: She takes into consideration the needs of the student and creates a learning environment in the classroom that will help each child grow. With her in-depth knowledge of subjects, students, pedagogy, and educational growth, she makes informed and wise decisions in the interest of children or youth. Another characteristic of the wise teacher is mentioned by Dewey: The wise teacher draws on the knowledge of experts as well as her own knowledge as she seeks to understand which particulars in the environment will best facilitate the development of each student. Dewey's emphasis is clear: We will not denigrate the knowledge of either the expert or the practitioner if we are wise. Both sources of knowledge—expert and experiential—are necessary if we are going to have a rich basis for making professional judgments. But we cannot be naïve about either source: We should filter the ideas of the expert as well as our own ideas to find and use the gems of each.

When thinking, then, Dewey implies that the teacher neither dismisses the interests of students nor sticks strictly to a prescribed curriculum or preconceived agenda. Nor does she abandon her responsibilities as a professional and leave decisions entirely up to students. She clearly understands that impulses and interests have to be "wisely supplemented" by a thoughtfully prepared learning environment and guided into appropriate activities (LW 17: 215–216). Likewise, she doesn't reject the best available thinking, theory, and research in favor of doing what she has always done. Let's stop to think about that phrase "what she has always done." Positively speaking, there are probably many things that we have always done that we ought to keep doing: reading research, reflecting on our teaching, preparing for our classes, caring for

> ### A Teacher Snapshot
>
> Using Dewey's thoughts about a wise teacher, describe a former teacher's decision that reflected considerable discretion.
>
> What did you notice about her thinking or behavior that impressed you? Do you know teachers who are not characterized by prudence? How would you describe their effect on students? parents? colleagues?

our students, imagining different ways to solve problems, thinking critically about issues, and so on. Negatively speaking, even good habits—not to mention sterile and counterproductive ones—can become unexciting, dull, and deadening for the student and teacher. The teacher may suffer most from the repetitive and unreflective use of good habits, but, of course, the student suffers too. Great artists detect when they are losing their enthusiasm by doing the same thing at the same time in the same way. They create alternative ways of enlivening their work and reaching their audiences. The wise teacher, therefore, cannot keep teaching the same way if she wants to stay emotionally and artistically alive.

Moreover, the wise teacher does not abandon her own experientially learned, reflectively analyzed, and critically evaluated beliefs just because she learns about new theories, studies, or practices. She has the good sense or wisdom to avoid pedagogical bandwagons, instructional merry-go-rounds, curricular hearses, and educational graveyards by thinking through experiences, theories, and research. She develops a reflective, evidentially based philosophy and practice of education. Children's whims, institutional traditions, colleague pressures, community preferences, and political ideologies are not allowed to throw or, at least, keep her off balance and direct her away from a thoughtful approach to meeting the legitimate interests of students, including their developing skills, values, understandings, and dispositions that are useful both now and in the future. She thinks about and chooses from educational studies and theories—as well as pedagogical mudslides and potholes—those ideas that are consistent with the reflective thought and practice she is continually enhancing, refining, and reconstructing. She has a passion for understanding and creating ever-better learning opportunities for her students.

Still, the wise teacher, like the wise parent, is much more. She has the insight and courage to act in the best interest of each child, even when a child prefers to be entertained or amused, for she understands that it is important to develop dispositions of perseverance in the face of distracting inclinations and wishes. More precisely, Dewey states in *Interest and Effort* (1913) that there is a need for the teacher to cultivate a continuity of effort on the part of students, particularly when learning is challenging or demanding:

> A judicious parent will not like to see a child too easily discouraged by meeting obstacles. If the child is physically healthy, surrender of a course of action, or diversion of energy to some easier line of action, is a bad symptom if it shows itself at the first sign of resistance. The demand for effort is a demand for *continuity* in the face of difficulties. (MW 7: 174–175)

Interest and effort need to be brought together as the child learns to keep pursuing difficult tasks that enable her to grow in the present and the future?

Does Dewey actually say that? If so, why doesn't he emphasize this point with some of the pedagodmothers and pedagodfathers who seem to think we can slip by the minds, emotions, and wills of students into their electrical centers to rewire them? Maybe he does, but perhaps they don't want to think there is any degree of student accountability. Regardless, we can listen to him. The wise teacher's role in soliciting the student's interest and effort and nurturing the student's engagement in educative experiences is one of her most essential undertakings.

In summary, Dewey envisions a teacher who is like a wise parent, who is capable of making informed, difficult, and intelligent judgments—an important set of abilities that Dewey wants every reflective person to possess (LW 8: 214–215)—about both her classroom and each student and who behaves in the light of her intelligently formed habits (LW 13: 18–19). Unsurprisingly, he notes that the capacity for judgment—the ability to solve identified problems by caringly selecting and thoughtfully appraising experience and data—distinguishes the artist from the person who is likely to make an intellectual mess of things (LW 8: 214). His distinction between the problem solver and the mess maker is a critical point for the teacher to grasp. Although this ability to make professional judgments distinguishes the artistic educator from the pedagogical bungler, it is unfortunately one of the last qualities many people—including some administrators, board members, guardians, parents, and policymakers—are willing for a teacher to employ regularly. Instead, many prefer a teacher who will somehow attempt to follow all of the contradictory demands that people attempt to force on her. Sadly, this "wooden and perfunctory pedagogue," as Dewey describes her, is often cherished more than the teacher who is characterized by energy, enthusiasm, passion, and "emotional and imaginative perception" (LW 10: 267). Too many of us are afraid of the latter kind of teacher.

Why do you think there is such a great fear of the thinking, feeling, and imaginative educator? Is it because people are so afraid of mess makers that they will not even tolerate the messy artist? No doubt, the artist is messy at times, but if she is wise, she isn't a mess maker. Nothing is wrong with being messy, of course, if it doesn't negatively affect educative learning experiences. Untidy or not, the artistic teacher avoids some problems and solves others—and enlists students to help her with these challenges. The wooden teacher cannot do either well and, therefore, she does not. Plus, if Dewey's poem, "Education," is correct, the wooden teacher uses some of the leftover timber from which she was chiseled to hull the mind of each student "with stiff well seasoned boards/brought from dry scholastic hoards" (Boydston, 1977, p. 52).

These ideas illustrate part of Dewey's conception of the teacher as wise mother. Yet the teacher is not the child's parent, and the school is not the student's home, although it often has to do things that some parents fail to do. Even so, significant distinctions between the two institutions and the parent and teacher need to remain clear. But a closing point of comparison that draws the community into the scenario with the parent and teacher deserves our reflection: "What the best and wisest parent wants for his own child, that must the community want for all of its children. Any other ideal for our schools is narrow and unlovely; acted upon, it destroys our democracy" (MW 1: 5). Does this thought suggest that what the best and wisest teacher wants for her own children every teacher should want—and seek—for all children?

QUOTES AND QUESTIONS

So far, we have looked at Dewey's ideas of art as an activity and as a product. We need now to consider the work of art and an aesthetic experience. First, we should understand that for Dewey *the* work of art is not the same thing as *a* work of art or an art product. A work of art is an object, an artistic product. *The* work or function of art is *what the product does in* the experience of an individual or society (LW 10: 113, 167). He claims that a genuinely aesthetic experience is a transformative one that makes the audience or perceiver or student and the environment "so fully integrated that each disappears" from consciousness. Applied to an aesthetically educative experience, the student or perceiver becomes so deeply engaged in an exploratory, creative, dialogical, or imaginative interaction that her awareness is largely limited to the experience itself (LW 10: 254). The absorption into, interaction with, and enjoyment of a product of art and the power of the experience is so moving that the student sees and acts differently in the future. This is its educational potential. It is transformative. One's perception, thinking, and feeling—indeed, one's life—are broadened and enriched by it. Art does its work in us (LW 10: 45ff). Although Dewey believes that this kind of aesthetic experience is too infrequent in schools, he thinks that it need not be rare; indeed, authentically artistic teaching is accompanied by just such experiences.

Here we should ask what Dewey means by his frequently used term *experience*, although we will return to the concept in a later chapter. Briefly stated, we may identify Dewey's definition of experience as those activities that involve both active and passive elements. The active side of experience involves the person doing something, and the passive side involves undergoing the consequences of our actions. The interaction of the person and her environment leads to change and learning: "We do something to the thing and then it does something to us in return." Experience, however, involves more than activity and more than change. It involves learning that consciously connects consequences with the initial activity or action (MW 9: 146). Later we shall see that Dewey enriches the idea. For now, we move to his idea of *an* experience, because it assists in clarifying both the notions of experience and aesthetic experience:

> We have *an* experience when the material experienced runs its course to fulfillment. Then and then only is it integrated within and demarcated in the general stream of experience from other experiences. A piece of work is finished in a way that is satisfactory; a problem receives its solution; a game is played through; a situation, whether that of eating a meal, playing a game of chess, carrying on a conversation, writing a book, or taking part in a political campaign, is so rounded out that its close is a consummation and not a cessation. Such an experience is a whole and carries with it its own individualizing quality and self-sufficiency. It is *an* experience. (LW 10: 42)

Think for a moment about how *an* aesthetic experience is related to the activity, product, and work of art and how all of these are related to the teacher being similar to a wise parent and an artist. First, let's examine the "doing" or activity aspect of the art of teaching. Is this kind of doing something the teacher does by herself? Or is it largely a social experience or activity? Or both? Can it be compared to a symphony and a conductor performing or working together? If it is a social experience, then the teacher and the students are involved together in the art of teaching. Of course, there are opportunities that call for the art of teaching in a one-on-one situation and in designing personalized studies, but even these have some social dimensions.

Second, the product aspect of the art of teaching involves both teacher and students, too. Students and teachers are co-learners, co-teachers, and co-creators. Thus, the product of independently thinking, choosing, and functioning students is also a social, collaborative experience. Interestingly, there are at least two ways to understand a product of art in the field of teaching: the process of becoming an educated person and the outcome of an educated person. These two—the process and the product—may be compared to a masterful performance by a symphony orchestra in Carnegie Hall and a masterpiece housed in the Louvre. The former is similar to fully engaged students who are participating in a performing art. The latter is like an educated graduate who is a culminating art product. Thus, a product of art that is a performance can, in a way, be simultaneously both an activity and product.

So, the teacher needs to address a number of artistic questions. How does the performing art (the activities of teaching and learning) assist in developing the final although dynamic product (the educated person)? In what ways is the former art related to the latter? How does a teacher know when a student is engrossed in a project and when she is simply daydreaming? Is there time for the class to truly have experiences and *an* experience, or must we be satisfied with isolated learning occurrences and move on to other prescribed objectives? Are group discussions educative or meandering? Will the immediate artistic activities sufficiently move the class toward the general educational product? In true artistic fashion, the art of thinking about these and other questions "proceeds neither by rule nor yet blindly" (LW 10: 125). The moment-by-moment reflection of the artist is required for delightful, rewarding outcomes.

Third, the work of art, if successful, must involve students' personal engagement and aesthetic satisfaction, but such stimulating, moving, engrossing, and enlarging experiences cannot be rushed. So how can we help students piece together or integrate the occasional and episodic learning moments so that more holistic experiences, *an* experience, and, especially, aesthetic experiences are more likely for students? Do summative discussions and experiences need to be better planned? Or are final art products largely by-products of concentrating on the doing aspect of art? Do we leave these experiences to chance or cultivate them? Or are both chance—or at least the unpredictable—and cultivation involved?

IMPLICATIONS FOR THE TEACHER

At this point, we could examine a wide range of ideas that have implications for the teacher, but we'll select just two of them. First, we will look at a largely neglected but still important idea: wisdom. The teacher, in Dewey's mind, needs to be wise just as much as the mother. In "Philosophy and Democracy"

(1919), Dewey tells us what wisdom is: It is not knowledge, not even a lot of knowledge, that is systematically arranged in a person's mind. Instead, it is

> a moral term, and like every moral term refers not to the constitution of things already in existence, not even if that constitution be magnified into eternity and absoluteness. As a moral term it refers to a choice about something to be done, a preference for living this sort of life rather than that. It refers not to accomplished reality but to a desired future which our desires, when translated into articulate conviction, may help bring into existence. (MW 11:44)

If we apply Dewey's idea of wisdom to the classroom and talk about the wise teacher, it is clear that wisdom should be involved in making decisions about teaching. Going back to the wise parent, we, at a minimum, see her making decisions about balancing the needs of the child with learning from the external environment; valuing both expert opinion and reflective experiential knowledge; adapting the best that the home has to offer regarding teaching and learning; providing individual opportunities for each child to develop her language, beliefs, and perceptions; and cultivating a desirable blend of interest and effort. These choices, Dewey maintains, are moral ones because they are choices about what the parent or teacher thinks a home or classroom should be, how she should teach, and how children or youth should learn. In *How We Think*, he links wisdom and the school curriculum and argues for nurturing wisdom in students:

> The distinction between information and wisdom is old, and yet requires constantly to be redrawn. Information is knowledge that is merely acquired and stored up; wisdom is knowledge operating in the direction of powers to the better living of life. Information, merely as information, implies no special training of intellectual capacity; wisdom is the finest fruit of that training. In school, amassing information always tends to escape from the ideal of wisdom or good judgment. (LW 8: 163)

Following Dewey, we will want to create situations and opportunities in which students are able to move beyond both information and knowledge to using their understanding for the betterment of school and their communities. With this knowledge, it is easy to understand the connection he makes in *Moral Principles in Education* (1909) between education and moral development. All education is unavoidably moral to the degree that it motivates students to live and conduct their lives in specific ways (MW 4: 267).

Second, we can now return to the transformative element in Dewey's idea of an aesthetic experience. Recall that he believes that an aesthetic experience entails the integration of the student into a learning experience and the fulfilling of that experience in such a manner that it is satisfying, rounded out, or completed. The experience stands or is seen as a whole and enables the student to think more broadly, deeply, and richly. The aesthetic learning experience is critical in the transformation of individual pieces of information and slices of knowledge into the life of the student. If the teacher is fortunate, she too enjoys the experience with the student.

What, however, can we do to nurture these transformative experiences? To begin, it may be wise to admit that genuinely aesthetic experiences are probably not everyday occurrences and that many times, they appear to be serendipitous and unpredictable. If we zealously attempt to create them for our students and ourselves, we will no doubt approach the endeavor incorrectly. These experiences are partly the result of living richly and fully in educative settings. Extrapolating from this concept of living richly and fully may mean that one of the most appropriate ways to cultivate aesthetic experiences is to create fertile learning environments and opportunities for students. As we attend to these things, experiences flow more easily and regularly, for "an experience is a product, one might almost say a by-product, of continuous and cumulative interaction of an organic self with the world" (LW 10: 224). And, finally, we must remember that the student, like the beholder of a great work, "must *create* his own experience" by interacting with the environment (LW 10: 60). Experience, like learning, is a personal matter for the student. Consequently, the well-prepared student is more likely to create enjoyable experiences of various kinds—what Dewey calls experience, *an* experience, and aesthetic experience—than one who enters a potentially educative experience unprepared or underprepared.

As wise parents know, there are things we can do to encourage and promote different kinds of experiences. Perhaps we can begin by revisiting former experiences to determine what we think led up to them and ask a set of questions. Were there prior studies, activities, or conversations that paved the way? Was the amount of time devoted to the experiences longer than usual? Were there specific group dynamics or a certain group size that contributed significantly? What was happening in the student or students as the experience unfolded? Was there a special theme that prompted attention? What times of the school year are these experiences most common? least common? Next, we may want to discuss the topic with other teachers to help us identify reasons for experiences, including *an* experience and aesthetic experiences. Plus, we may want to think of our individual aesthetic experiences in museums or theaters or on beaches or country roads. What role did the prior readings, discussions, and viewings have in helping create the experiences? Think of the influence of different docents on these experiences. What did they do at the beginning, along the way, and at the end that led to our being engrossed in the experience?

Of course, your own questions will touch your experiences in ways no one else can imagine. So why not begin your own questioning and answering now?

A SUMMATIVE EXERCISE

Chapter 4   The Teacher as Wise Mother

Understandings	*Qualities*	*Activities*

READINGS

"Education." (1977). In J. A. Boydston (Ed.), *The Poems of John Dewey* (pp. 51–53). Carbondale: Southern Illinois University Press.
"The Classroom Teacher" (MW 15: 180–189).
"Having an Experience" in *Art as Experience* (LW 10: 42–63).
"What Is Thinking?" in *How We Think: A Restatement of the Relation of Reflective Thinking to the Educative Process* (LW 8: 113–124).

FIVE

The Teacher as Navigator

Since learning is something that the pupil has to do himself and for himself, the initiative lies with the learner. The teacher is a guide and director; he steers the boat but the energy that propels it must come from those who are learning.

—John Dewey (LW 8: 140)

A nother analogy? Well, this time Dewey gives us several in one sentence. He explicitly likens the teacher to a guide and a director and implicitly compares her to a helmsman and a navigator in the quoted extract from *How We Think* (1933). These analogies are probably woven together in his thinking, although there may be distinctive elements in each. We decided to use the word *navigator*, because we think it can cover all three major concepts, namely guiding, directing, and steering. On the other hand, we could miss an emphasis, probably the main emphasis, of Dewey's statement if we focus exclusively on

Authors' Note: References to works by John Dewey are from the collection of his works published by Southern Illinois University Press: *The Early Works of John Dewey, 1882–1898; The Middle Works of John Dewey, 1899–1924;* and *The Later Works of John Dewey, 1925–1953.* References to these works are abbreviated as EW, MW, and LW, where, for example, EW 5: 94 indicates that the material cited or idea noted is in *The Early Works,* Volume 5, page 94.

the teacher and ignore the student. He obviously wants us to understand three enormously important overlapping thoughts about the learner.

What are these thoughts? Before we answer this question, let's observe that the ideas cluster around the notions of learning and learner and convey beliefs about the student that are found infrequently in much contemporary educational literature. The first notion that Dewey stresses is that learning is something a student does and does for herself. Learning is an activity and, as such, is an engagement that may result in educative experiences by a student. The teacher can do her own learning in an educative manner, but she cannot learn for the student. She plays critical roles in the learning process of the student, but, ultimately, only the student can learn for herself. No amount of preparation or, even, enticement, therefore, by the teacher can secure learning without the active involvement of the student. The student, in a sense, is in charge of learning. There are times when this realization can be reassuring, just as it can be sobering.

This isn't the whole picture, however.

The second piece of news, good news if you think a particular way, from Dewey is that the impetus and initiative for learning innately resides in the child or youth. This news, of course, is not claiming that the teacher and school are insignificant. On the contrary, they are vital factors that affect the learning activities of students. But the teacher and the school are not alone in their interest in learning. They have a ready, interested collaborator in the learning process, the student. The student is not only interested in learning. She actually seeks to learn. Her initiative stems from what Dewey considers her original and cultivated impulses to learn. All of these tendencies to learn, of course, need to be nurtured and guided by the teacher and sustained by the student. Remember, nevertheless, that the student independently has the initiative to learn. If Dewey is correct on this point, important ideas flow from it: The teacher and student and other students become partners—co-partners— in the learning process. Dewey asks us to abandon any ideas that imply that the student is passive and disinterested in learning. Instead, she is an active, searching person (MW 7: 251). But we have to think of each student as an individual learner and decide how we can wisely guide her in the role of a co-partner or co-learner. Dewey identifies two steps in this process: establishing educative conditions and sharing educative activities:

> Setting up conditions which stimulate certain visible and tangible ways of acting is the first step. Making the individual a sharer or partner in the associated activity so that he feels its success as his success, its failure as his

failure, is the completing step. As soon as he is possessed by the emotional attitude of the group, he will be alert to recognize the special ends at which it aims and the means employed to secure success. His beliefs and ideas, in other words, will take a form similar to those of others in the group. He will also achieve pretty much the same stock of knowledge since that knowledge is an ingredient of his habitual pursuits. (MW 9: 18)

We just said that we need to consider each student's distinct dispositions and abilities so that we can wisely guide her into the role of a learning co-partner. In light of what Dewey says are the two steps of guidance, we may wish to revise our statement to "wisely and *ethically* guide her," especially since—as we learned earlier—Dewey thinks making wise decisions is a moral undertaking. Wisdom is needed to create conditions or an environment that will stimulate and direct the learning activities of a student, but a respect for the integrity and autonomy of the student is required if we want to create independently thinking and choosing people, not just students who absorb the attitudes and behaviors of their classmates. Take a moment to notice Dewey's reference to a "stock of knowledge." He believes we need a stock of knowledge that can be used in problem solving. He isn't interested in our graduating empty-minded students or students who cannot reflect on problems and issues, because they have neither a stock of knowledge nor a means of acquiring relevant information.

The third thing Dewey tells us is also delightful: that our learning vessel has its own fuel. The student has her own unending or renewal supply of energy and, as a result, there is no dependency on imported energy—just imported wisdom and guidance. She isn't, then, just the initiator of learning, she is also the energizer for the entire educational journey. Now, for the not-necessarily-so-good news: A student can initiate and energize learning in any number of directions, inappropriate and appropriate. Cruises upstream and downstream, trips across oceans and back again, and voyages from port to port can result in noneducative, uneducative, miseducative, and educative experiences (MW 7: 178; LW 13: 17–30). These four options are illustrated in Table 5.1.

> **A Teacher Snapshot**
>
> Recall a few school incidents that remind you of what Dewey says about educative, miseducative, uneducative, and noneducative experiences. Was it the teacher's navigation that made the most difference in educative experiences? What other factors were involved?

Table 5.1   Types of Learning Experiences

Types	Explanations	Examples
Noneducative	Learning or activity that leads to little or no immediate understanding and little or no growth in the future	Memorizing a name, date, or formula; learning to skip rope or sharpen a pencil
Uneducative	Learning or activity that fails to clarify educational ends and consider appropriate means for seeking ends	Studying history or literature without reflecting on personal or social purposes and relevant methods of inquiry
Miseducative	Learning or activity that is based on misunderstandings, confusion, or unethical behavior and that results in future misinterpretations	Picking up derogatory language and images of an ethnic, racial, or religious group
Educative	Learning that provides intellectual and moral growth in the present and the grounds for more growth in the future	Engaging in activities that provide understandings that prove useful in addressing present and future personal and social problems

A navigator, therefore, needs to know where the educative ports are located and how these ports may be entered most successfully by each student. The analogies of guiding, directing, and steering may now make more sense: Teachers are needed to ensure that energized students take educative excursions, voyages that are growth-producing, growth-enhancing, and empowering for the students.

You may be wondering if Dewey is going to take us on a cruise of our own, perhaps to visit Delight Elementary School, Enchanting Middle School, or Fantasy High School where students happily paddle along with their teachers on their pleasant pedagogical pilgrimages. Teaching, after all, is easy when we know the truth. Or is this the story that Dewey tells? He no doubt takes flights of fantasy now and then. But in his better moments, he stresses that the propensities of the student present challenges and that his view of teaching is more demanding than traditional approaches, not less (LW 13: 50). Left to herself, he recognizes that the student is unlikely to progress from native or socially shaped impulses to conscious desires and reflective purposes. The ignored, isolated, or spoiled student will be at the mercy of undeveloped inclinations and indiscriminate stimuli (LW 13: 43ff). A navigator, therefore, cannot carelessly allow a student's impulses to drive her onto educational shoals or over falls. Nor can she abandon the student to the stimuli and forces of an accidental or spontaneous environment. Miseducative shipwrecks are not an option for the caring teacher.

In *Ethics* (revised 1932), Dewey pulls together his thoughts about native impulses, environment, energy, and the educator:

> Stimuli from the environment are highly important factors in conduct. But they are not important as causes, as generators of action. For the organism is already active, and stimuli themselves arise and are experienced only in the course of action. The painful heat of an object stimulates the hand to withdraw but the heat was experienced in the course of reaching and exploring. The function of a stimulus is—as the case just cited illustrates—to change the direction of an action already going on. Similarly, a response to a stimulus is not the beginning of activity; it is a change, a shift, of activity in response to the change in conditions indicated by a stimulus. A navigator of a ship perceives a headland; this may operate to make him alter the course which his ship takes.
>
> But it is not the cause or "moving spring" of his sailing. Motives, like stimuli, induce us to alter the trend and course of our conduct, but they do not evoke or originate action as such. (LW 7: 289–290)

Dewey's comments convey important subtleties about both the student and the teacher. The former does not need stimuli or motives to cause her to become active. Her fuel tank is full; she is already active; her engine is running; she is moving in some direction. While she is moving, the stimuli draw or repel her and are selected or ignored by her. When a stimulus or motive is selected by the student, because it creates questions, presents a problem, or generates disequilibrium for her, it works to direct her attention and learning. The teacher indirectly directs the student by prior planning of trips, presentation of possibilities, selection of materials, creation of activities, construction of centers, placement of stimuli, design of questions, scheduling of projects, and provision of opportunities. The teacher also recognizes a "headland" that influences her to adjust plans and redirect the vessel to an unanticipated opportunity that leads to consummating aesthetic experiences. Together—the learner (teacher) and the co-learner (student)—have experiences that provide growth in the present and create opportunities for future development. The entire sequence of events, then, may be—if a positive scenario is described—as follows when viewed from a distance: Native impulses lead to instinctive or planned activity and are influenced by environmental stimuli as a child or youth learns to respond to the environment and select new directions or activities. The entire process is infused with ethical decisions or selections by both the teacher and the student as they work and grow together.

What, then, do Dewey's analogies of the teacher as guide, director, and navigator suggest? Plainly stated, the teacher steers a vessel where she thinks it should go while considering the purposes of the craft. But this cannot be done if the teacher doesn't understand the student and her purposes. Dewey, as we might expect, offers us more than a path to understanding the student as he provides invaluable insight about what the teacher needs to know about each student, the process of education, and the general direction of education:

> The more a teacher is aware of the past experiences of students, of their hopes, [and] chief interests, the better will he understand the forces at work that need to be directed and utilized for the formation of reflective habits. The number and quality of these factors vary from person to person. They cannot therefore be categorically enumerated in a book. But there are some tendencies and forces that operate in every normal individual, forces that must be appealed to and utilized if the best methods of development of good habits of thought are to be employed. (LW 8: 141)

Understanding students and guiding, directing, and steering them to develop reflective habits, therefore, says a great deal but not all about Dewey's thinking. In his opinion, we need to take hold of student impulses, curiosities, and interests and assist them as they grow into independent thinkers and productive individuals. In this process, Dewey makes a case for getting students to move beyond their immediate personal interests of merely being thinking and productive people. We need to steer them toward social concerns, sympathies, and involvements. With appropriate social moorings, they can be active participants in building, expanding, and sustaining democratic policies, institutions, communities, and governments (MW 9: 154–155)—all of which in turn mean richer lives for those involved.

QUOTES AND QUESTIONS

In another context, Dewey uses a different nautical metaphor that has applicability to our analysis of the teacher. He argues that a nautical almanac—whose parallel we might see in a curriculum guide, university course, district workshop, or teacher preparation program—however informative, cannot tell the sailor where he is nor how to navigate. It is an aid in his analysis of the required conditions of right navigation. In the supreme art of life the tools must be less mechanical; more depends upon the skill of the artists in their manipulation, but they are none the less useful. Our mastery of a required case of action would be slow and wavering if we had to forge anew our weapons of attack in each instance. The temptation to fall back on the impulse or accident of the moment would be well-nigh irresistible. And so it is well we have our rules at hand, but well only if we have them for use. (EW 3: 101)

> **A Reflective Opportunity**
>
> If you were designing a set of activities to cultivate the moment-by-moment thinking that Dewey urges, how would they differ from many of your past education or development experiences? Are these differences consistent with what Dewey suggests? That is, are your means consistent with your goals?

Unpacking this statement by Dewey is worth the endeavor, for he implies much about how the teacher who is an artist thinks and how prior learning and experience can help or hinder our efforts in new pedagogical circumstances. What does he say that is most meaningful to you as an aspiring or practicing teacher? Do you think he is correct when he adds that an educational rule or principle does not tell us how to act or teach in a specific situation but does provide "a most marvelous tool of analysis" and assists in clearing away distracting matters (EW 3: 101)? Can you think of an example to illustrate your point?

Before going to the next chapter, examining briefly a different but pertinent analogy is important. The reason we think it is important may seem like an unusual one: We think Dewey is dead wrong. Okay, so he isn't dead, but he is incorrect or, at a minimum, incomplete because he stopped thinking too early. Let's look at what he says. In the same paragraph that Dewey speaks of the teacher as a guide, director, and navigator, he suggests that the teacher is also like a salesperson, claiming:

> Teaching may be compared to selling commodities. No one can sell unless someone buys. We should ridicule a merchant who said that he had sold a great many goods although no one had bought any. But perhaps there are teachers who think that they have done a good day's teaching irrespective of what pupils have learned. (LW 8: 140)

Today, we are all too familiar with this idea as well as the accompanying one that the student is similar to or actually a customer. The implications of this analogy or, perhaps, literalism appear to differ from writer to writer. Sometimes the salesperson illustration suggests that schools and districts are in competition with one another and that we need to compete for and keep students. A complementary idea is that the teacher needs to develop her art of selling the value of ideas and skills or schooling and education. Or the thought suggested may be that we need to know our merchandise (knowledge), our customers (students), and our sales approaches (methods) very well if we are to remain relevant and competitive in society today.

Dewey is not, however, speaking of these issues and ideas. He doesn't say the teacher is a salesperson and the student is a customer. Conversely, he is talking about the relationship between the concepts of teaching and learning and selling and buying. His very specific point is that we haven't taught if students haven't learned, just as a salesperson hasn't sold anything if customers haven't purchased anything. Or, more exactly, he dislikes the idea of our saying we have been teaching when our pupils' learning or lack thereof is ignored. Pupils need to be in the equation when we say that teaching has occurred.

This idea doesn't sound bad. But Dewey did not see how his idea might be misapplied. Thus, we may want to question whether it confuses as much as it enlightens. For example, isn't there an *attempt* sense to selling and teaching as well as a *success* sense? Don't we speak of both teaching and selling even if students haven't learned and customers haven't purchased? Should we expect a salesperson to answer the question, "What have you been doing today?" with "Nothing," if she didn't sell any computers? And what has a teacher been doing if not teaching when students fail to learn? Has she been doing nothing? And if 2 students don't learn but 23 others do, has the teacher failed or succeeded at teaching? Or both? This analogy also illustrates that any comparison may be misleading or only partially correct: Things are alike only to a certain extent. Part of the art of thinking rests "in the power to pass judgments *pertinently* and *discriminatingly*" (LW 8: 211). And to be a good, critically thinking judge

> is to have a sense of the relative indicative or signifying values of the various features of the perplexing situation; to know what to let go as of no account; what to eliminate as irrelevant; what to retain as conducive to the outcome; what to emphasize as a clew to the difficulty. This power in ordinary matters we call *knack, tact, cleverness*; in more important affairs, *insight, discernment*. In part it is instinctive or inborn, but it also represents the funded outcome of long familiarity with like operations in the past. Possession of this ability to seize what is evidential or significant and to let the rest go is the mark of the expert. The connoisseur, the *judge*, in any matter. (LW 8: 213)

Only with an understanding of education that is based in or funded by pertinent bodies of knowledge and experiential understanding is the teacher well on her way to being prepared to become a pedagogical artist, for great teaching demands great thinking and imagination (LW 10: 52). Both thinking and imagination necessitate the teacher's becoming a judge and critic of what she reads, hears, sees, and does (MW 3: 260).

IMPLICATIONS FOR THE TEACHER

Navigating 25 to say nothing of 150 students each day is no simple matter. Guiding their interests, choices, and learning can be unbelievably challenging as the substitute and new teacher soon discover. Steering students in their acquisition of meaningful information and critical thinking—so that they attend to relevant factors and evaluate their meanings—calls for a great artist. The joys of teaching, then, require the joys—and sometimes traumas—of thinking. And not just thinking but thinking in such a way that it becomes part of our practice and shapes what we do as if it were second nature. Each teacher must think through issues, questions, and choices so that she is distinguished by having "pedagogical horse sense," as Dewey suggests:

> Judging is the act of selecting and weighing the bearing of facts and suggestions
> as they present themselves, as well as of deciding whether the alleged facts are
> really facts and whether the idea used is a sound idea or merely a fancy. We
> may say, for short, that a person of sound judgment is one who, in the idiomatic
> phrase, has 'horse sense'; he is a good judge of *relative values*; he can estimate,
> appraise, evaluate, with tact and discernment. (LW 8: 210)

This is how a teacher's knowledge transforms her practice and why we are able
to say that theory and practice go together.

The teacher as a navigator, then, brings us face to face with several arts,
including the art of thinking. Dewey hints at the beauty of this art:

> Thinking is preeminently an art; knowledge and propositions which are
> the products of thinking, are works of art, as much so as statuary and sym-
> phonies. Every successive stage of thinking is a conclusion in which the
> meaning of what has produced it is condensed; and it is no sooner stated than
> it is a light radiating to other things—unless it be a fog which obscures them.
> (LW 1: 283)

But thinking can be otherwise:

> In some cases the result is called unworthy, in others, ugly; in others, inept;
> in others, wasteful, inefficient; and in still others untrue, false. But in each
> case, the condemnatory adjective refers to the resulting work judged in the
> light of its method of production. (LW 1: 284)

Accordingly, thinking can be done well or poorly, as can our navigating.
As teachers, we need to think—sorry about that word—and plan carefully so
we can be at our intellectual and pedagogical best. We should cultivate the art
of thinking as a part of the art of teaching. Moreover, we need to think like
artists if we want to perform like them. What we do is too important to individual, group, national, and world progress to do otherwise. As we refine our artistic thinking, we find little help and no escape in traditional practices, approved
textbooks, teacher-proof materials, or mandated curricula. On the other hand,
teacher education programs, graduate studies, and other professional development activities ought to help us think more rigorously, critically, richly, and
comprehensively—and, hence, more artistically. If they do, but especially if
they don't, we need to find similarly minded artists to help us think beautiful
thoughts and practice them in our classrooms and schools so that life and
learning become "a never ending voyage of discovery" (LW 11: 502).

To be sure, teaching artistically is not the only or even the primary factor in developing the kinds of educated people and democratic societies we find desirable. A great teacher, even an educationally powerful school, is only one means to a more desirable community, society, and world. Just how influential a good teacher is is impossible to determine. We can safely assert, however, that she is both very important for individuals and communities and not significant enough to cure or avoid depressions, diseases, wars, poverty, injustice, and tragedy. Dewey confesses in *Democracy and Education*, "Schools are, indeed, one important method of the transmission which forms the dispositions of the immature; but it is only one means, and compared with other agencies, a relatively superficial means" (MW 9: 7). Yet, we dare not underestimate the potential of schools and teachers. Isn't it better to fly artistically toward high ideals than to skim the treetops because of low expectations?

A SUMMATIVE EXERCISE

Chapter 5   The Teacher as Navigator

Understandings	*Qualities*	*Activities*

READINGS

"The Philosophy of the Arts," (LW 13: 357–368).
"The Place of Judgment in Reflective Activity," in *How We Think* (LW 8: 210–220).
"The Varied Substance of the Arts," in *Art as Experience* (LW 10: 218–249).

SIX

The Teacher
as Gardener

While the raw material and the starting-point of growth are found in native capacities, the environing conditions to be furnished by the educator are the indispensable means of their development. They are not, and do not of themselves decide, the end. A gardener, a worker of metals, must observe and pay attention to the properties of his material. If he permits these properties in their original form to dictate his treatment, he will not get anywhere. If they decide his end, he will fixate raw materials in their primitive state. Development will be arrested, not promoted. He must bring to his consideration of his material an idea, an ideal, of possibilities not realized, which must be in line with the constitution of his plant or ore; it must not do violence to them; it must be their possibilities.

—John Dewey (LW 9: 197–198)

W hen was the last time you grew some tomatoes, planted a tree, fertilized your lawn, or watered your houseplants? Recently, we hope.

Authors' Note: References to works by John Dewey are from the collection of his works published by Southern Illinois University Press: *The Early Works of John Dewey, 1882–1898; The Middle Works of John Dewey, 1899–1924;* and *The Later Works of John Dewey,* 1925–1953. References to these works are abbreviated as EW, MW, and LW, where, for example, EW 5: 94 indicates that the material cited or idea noted is in *The Early Works,* Volume 5, page 94.

Having some experience as a home gardener, a metal worker, or a farmer will make this chapter more meaningful as well as enable you to think through the limitations of these analogies. Ideally, they will allow you to see parallels between gardening and teaching that would otherwise go unseen. We can also learn a great deal from Dewey's analysis. So, let's examine what he says. We will notice two of his related analogies—the metalworker and the farmer—as we devote most of our attention to his idea of the gardener.

We begin by looking at three of Dewey's key beliefs:

1. the student's native capacities are the starting point of educational gardening and growing,

2. the educational environment is the means of developing native capacities, and

3. the educator is to provide the educational environment to nourish the student's native abilities.

Hidden in the first belief is a reference to his concept of growth. So, another belief that may be distinguished from the other three is that

4. the unending goal of education is growth. Indeed, education is seen as growth, and growth is seen as education (LW 13: 19).

These four ideas will be analyzed in turn. First, the raw material or student—whatever the stage of development she is in at the time a teacher works with a child or adolescent—is the starting point of growth. Note that Dewey says the starting point, not the whole or only concern. Implicit in this statement is Dewey's idea that the curriculum needs to be adapted to the student's developmental stage or growth level, which is influenced by both her psychological maturation and social enculturation. Contrary to what some claim, however, he isn't recommending an individualistic, child-centered approach to education. Conversely, he sees the child as a social being learning in a community: "The *process* of mental development is essentially a social process of participation" (LW 11: 206). Even the individual student's educational plan is contributed to by "all engaged in the learning process," including the teacher, who leads the social group or class in "the process of [creating a] social intelligence" (LW 13: 47). On the other hand, he recognizes that many educators have been and are overly focused on themselves as authority figures or on the course to be studied, which detracts from the importance of the learner in her social context. So he complains about these perspectives because they place

> the center of gravity . . . outside the child. It is in the teacher, the textbook, anywhere and everywhere you please except in the immediate instincts and activities of the child himself. On that basis there is not much to be said about the *life* of the child. A good deal might be said about the studying of the child, but the school is not the place where the child *lives*. Now the change which is coming into our education is the shifting of the center of gravity. It is a change, a revolution, not unlike that introduced by Copernicus when the astronomical center shifted from the earth to the sun. In this case, the child becomes the sun about which the appliances of education revolve; he is the center about which they are organized. (MW 1: 23)

Learning, therefore, needs to focus on the student in learning communities, not the curriculum, teacher, or the individual student in isolation. Observe that Dewey speaks of understanding the student by studying her in the context of where she *lives*, not studying her in the classroom (although he thinks doing this is also important). Dewey's thought on learning about the student engaged in the typical activities of life may rarely have been consistently practiced by a school faculty, much less the teaching staff of a district.[1] If we are really attempting to understand a student—especially one who presents behavioral or instructional challenges, but also any child we wish to know really well—how can we depend on the partial picture we have of her from the somewhat artificial classroom and school environments? Certainly, child and adolescent psychology can help us understand students, but we need to understand specific students, not just age-level and cultural norms. We might ask, therefore, how would we practice Dewey's ideas if we genuinely believe they are important? If we really believe children are invaluable? Is his hypothesis that understanding the student outside of class leads to better in-class learning for her worth testing? Or are you already familiar with educators and practices that throw light on this responsibility? If you know of such programs, what do they have to offer?

From prior discussions, it is obvious that Dewey thinks we should study our students. But we may think this studying is fundamentally learning about them as we teach. More is involved, however. Whether we are studying students in schools or in their neighborhoods, it is important to know what we are seeking to discover or learn, not just casually pick up isolated pieces of information during the day. When Dewey zeroes in on the child or youth, he

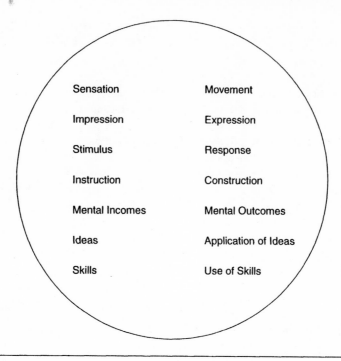

Sensation	Movement
Impression	Expression
Stimulus	Response
Instruction	Construction
Mental Incomes	Mental Outcomes
Ideas	Application of Ideas
Skills	Use of Skills

Figure 6.1   The Active Mind and the Learning Circle

thinks we need to begin with the assumption that the person is an active learner who is pushed by her impulses, desires, and purposes. Because learning is a continuous activity, the teacher can learn a great deal about the individual student in her cultural and classroom contexts by understanding what he terms the learning circle. Figure 6.1 captures some of his key ideas about the active mind and the circle.

From Dewey's perspective, learning is never fully complete until the active mind, sensations or stimuli, and movements or responses make a full circle. That is to say, learning doesn't fully occur unless a student is capable of understanding and applying the sensations felt, impressions experienced, ideas explored, and skills taught. If only one side of the circle is evident, there is no evidence that the student has learned. He thinks part of what we should study, then, is the way each student's experiencing is publicly and socially manifested: how she physically conducts herself after interacting with others, expresses the studied elements of the environment, responds to stimuli, constructs meanings, displays her thinking, applies ideas, and uses skills. This study of students is much like a gardener's painstaking examination of the visible responses of different kinds of flowers to sunlight and shade, heat and cold, drought and rain, and manufactured nutrients and natural ingredients. If we want healthy, flourishing, growing flowers—and students—we must understand them and how they are influenced by and respond to the activities and events of the environment.

A further word about responding to the environment from the perspective of Dewey's concept of experience seems appropriate. In any experience, as we noted earlier, he thinks there are two elements: the active side and the passive side. The active side includes the active mind and more, that is, the active person or her *doings*. The passive side refers to what she undergoes or her *undergoings*, or what happens to her as a result of her actions. The consequences of her actions result in undergoing change, discovering meaning, or, in essence, learning (MW 9: 146). In the context of the learning circle, the doings and undergoings of the student need to be followed by additional doings to make the circle complete. This kind of study that includes analyzing the student's active mind and experiences—doings, undergoings, and later doings—takes a great deal of time and results in knowledge that should not be discarded after nine months. Collectively, a group of gardeners will want to ensure that the information is used and updated in the schools that subsequently serve a student.

As we shall later see, this depiction of learning alone does not exhaust Dewey's theory, for he thinks the teacher needs to examine consciously more than the student's mind, the sensations or impressions that stimulate it, and the responses selected. But studying the student's inner thoughts, proclivities, and stimuli choices is a significant part of understanding the student. To ignore these matters either in or outside school will certainly mean the teacher remains an outsider to the life of the student. Her inner life needs to be studied in connection with its outer manifestations, and these expressions are partially seen in the student's activities while dealing with obstacles and solving problems. Figure 12.1, the Student's Cycle of Environmental Interaction (page 166, this volume) illustrates other parts of Dewey's theory of learning.

The second and third points—the educational environment is the means of developing native capacities, and the educator is to provide the educational environment for the student's development—are ideas that have been discussed before or which will be discussed later. Thus, we turn our attention to his fourth notion for the moment: The unending goal of education is growth. In his statement, Dewey observes that the gardener should not allow the original instincts of the student to determine or dictate the way the teacher facilitates learning or designs educational activities or environments. To do so would be to stymie growth rather than promote it and result in fixating on the undeveloped inclinations of students. Instead, the teacher should bring to the student an idea, ideal, or possibility not yet realized.Or, in terms of his earlier remark about the artist, the teacher needs to bring a vision of developing the student's abilities but at the same time respect the autonomy and individuality of the student. His phrase— "possibilities . . . must be in line with the constitution of his plant or ore; it must not do violence to them; it must be *their* possibilities" (LW 9: 197)—clarifies the need to honor the student, respect her strengths and inclinations, and work with powers and potentialities. Our purely personal visions—apart from the student, her capabilities and purposes, and ethical restrictions—are not to be imposed on the student. To return to the gardening metaphor, the teacher does not seek to force a student to be a literary, musical, or biological wizard any more than a gardener would seek to transform a desert cactus into a tropical flower. Nor would she seek to create a tropical environment for the student when she needs a semiarid one. The ideal or vision of the teacher, therefore, involves both the process or means and the end or aim of education.

An Introspective Moment

What is your vision of student development? of societal development? Are your visions consistent with a democratic philosophy of education?

The process of education has already been mentioned or alluded to on several occasions. Two additional comments are merited. Negatively, the process is circumscribed in at least two ways by Dewey. First, the process of education does not allow the student to merely pursue her undeveloped instincts or interests. Second, the process of education does not allow the teacher to impose her personal agenda on the student. Positively, the process is also prescribed in at least two respects. First, the process does call for the teacher's having a vision of where the development of the student's possibilities may lead. Second, the process involves ongoing growth; it is a dynamic process that is unending. Both the negative and positive dimensions of the process of education are related to the teacher's vision or ideals.

In *Experience and Education*, Dewey also clarifies that the teacher's ideals should be connected to educative experiences, which are characterized in part by student outcomes in the realm of knowledge:

- an understanding of more facts,
- an entertaining of more ideas, and
- a better intellectual arrangement of the learned facts and ideas (LW 13: 55).

The teacher's vision, therefore, should begin with the native abilities and social experiences of the student, but she should also guide the student into "a fuller and richer and also more organized form [of understanding], a form that gradually approximates that in which subject-matter is presented to the skilled, mature person" (LW 13: 48). Focusing on the student, then, means more than one thing to Dewey. Among other things, it means focusing on her native abilities and inclinations, social and cultural background, and intellectual and moral growth. Likewise, it means seeing the student as a growing social being who is respected as she develops her own purposes and goals and learns to make choices in the interest of others. Another developmental pattern appears, too: Native abilities should be developed through social experiences that result in a better understanding of subject matter.

Okay, so we know something of Dewey's beliefs about the student and the teacher and his ideas of the process, content, and end of education. But what does he mean by the concept of growth? A seed naturally grows into a cornstalk, maple tree, sandspur, or suchlike. But Dewey views human growth as somewhat different from that of a plant although he uses the analogy of the gardener. He identifies two major fallacies in adhering to *a naturalistic model of growth*, one that prescribes a number of teacher-student relationships:

> In the first place seed-growth is limited as compared with human growth; its future is much more prescribed by its antecedent nature; its line of growth is comparatively fixed; it has not the capacities for growth in different directions toward different outcomes characteristic of the human young, which is also, if you please, a seed embodying germinal powers but may develop any of many forms. (LW 9: 195)

A pine seedling may grow into an unhealthy or healthy tree, but its scope of growth is narrowly confined compared to that of a child, who may grow into a well or poorly developed teacher, terrorist, painter, pedophile, cosmetologist, or curmudgeon. In one sense, Dewey is suggesting that the growth of a tree is quite limited and finite and that the growth of the student is nearly unlimited and infinite. These radical differences mean that the potentialities of the student need much more attention and direction than the growth of plants.

Secondly, Dewey clarifies that natural growth is not necessarily as "natural" as some theorists suggest:

> Even the seed of a plant does not grow simply of itself without atmospheric aids. Its development is controlled by external conditions and forces. Native inherent forces must interact with external if there is to be life and development. In brief, development, even with a plant, depends on the kind of interaction between itself and its environment. A stunted oak, or a stalk of maize with few ears of scattered grains, exhibits natural development as truly as the noblest tree or the prize-winning ear of maize. The difference in result is due not only to native stock but also to environment; the finest native stock would come to an untimely end, or give a miserable product, if its own energies could not interact with favorable atmospheric conditions. (LW 9: 195–196)

Dewey's comments resonate if we've done any kind of gardening or farming. For example, try planting corn in eastern North Carolina and west Texas, or seek to grow potatoes on Prince Edward Island and in Newfoundland. The outcomes may be somewhat natural but they will also be significantly if not radically different and vary in desirability. Plants vary in their ability to grow in particular climates and soils, differ in their needs for water and sunlight, deviate in their requirements for thinning and pruning, and diverge in their profiting from fertilization and cultivation. Similarly, students as individuals respond differently to their environments, need different atmospheres sometimes, and profit from personalized treatment. The complexities of these demands bring us back to an earlier analogy and related quality, the wise parent who is capable of using her judgment to attend to the particular needs of each student. If she follows Dewey's thinking, she believes in directed growth rather than natural development.

QUOTES AND QUESTIONS

In *Democracy and Education*, Dewey introduces a complementary notion to the analogy of the teacher as gardener. That is, he compares the teacher to a farmer. Although long, the following quotation is worth examining:

There is nothing peculiar about educational aims. They are just like aims in any directed occupation. The educator, like the farmer, has certain things to do, certain resources with which to do, and certain obstacles with which to contend. The conditions with which the farmer deals, whether obstacles or resources, have their own structure and operation independently of any purpose of his. Seeds sprout, rain falls, the sun shines, insects devour, blight comes, the seasons change.

His aim is simply to utilize these various conditions; to make his activities and their energies work together, instead of against one another. It would be absurd if the farmer set up a purpose of farming, without any reference to these conditions of soil, climate, characteristics of plant growth, etc. His purpose is simply a foresight of the consequences of his energies connected with those of the things about him, a foresight used to direct his movements from day to day. Foresight of possible consequences leads to more careful and extensive observation of the nature and performances of the things he had to do with, and to laying out a plan—that is, of a certain order in the acts to be performed. (MW 9: 113–114)

Pick out some terms from this quote and consider them for a minute. Maybe they will be *aims, obstacles, consequences,* and *absurdity*? Maybe not. Perhaps you prefer to reflect on the implications of *purpose, foresight, direct,* or *plan*. Whatever your selection, you will see points of similarity between the teacher and farmer. Do you also see differences? How do these ideas inform your thinking? Do any suggest changes for your teaching? If so, what are the potential changes you should consider?

Dewey speaks further about a specific educational aim and combines this interest with his view of the development of individuals growing in a democratic school and society:

A Teacher Snapshot

Do you know a teacher who is genuinely artistic as she helps students understand their biases and prejudices? That is, is she ethical as she nurtures ethical growth and judgment? Which of her qualities are most obvious to you and others?

The aim of education is development of individuals to the utmost of their potentialities. But this statement as such leaves unanswered the question of the measure of the development to be desired and worked for. A society of free individuals in which all, in doing each his own work, contribute to the liberation and enrichment of the lives of others is the only environment for the normal growth to full stature. An environment in which some are limited will always in reaction create conditions that prevent the full development even of those who fancy they enjoy complete freedom for unhindered growth. (LW 9: 202–203)

Behind this comment, Dewey is concerned that a "wave of nationalistic sentiment, of racial and national prejudice, of readiness to resort to force of arms" (LW 9: 203) is plaguing society and schools. He goes further to say that "schools must have somehow failed grievously" because of this powerful wave of feelings being so widespread and powerful (LW 9: 203). Stop and think about what he is saying. How much do you think schools can be held accountable for the cultivation of a democratic society? How much do you think society influences schools to be undemocratic? Is Dewey correct in blaming schools for the lack of growth toward democratic ideals? If so, to what degree? If not, what is the role of the school in helping both students and society grow in the direction of democratic ideals?

IMPLICATIONS FOR THE TEACHER

We might wish to discuss numerous implications of Dewey's ideas, but there is limited time to examine them. Which one or two or three shall we select? Why don't we allow Dewey to identify an implication? In the essay "The Need for a Philosophy of Education" (1934), we have already had our attention drawn to the idea of the teacher as a gardener and a metal worker:

> The gardener and worker in metals may take as their measures results already achieved with plants and ores, although originality and invention will intro-duce some variation. But the true educator, while using results already accomplished cannot make them his final and complete standard. Like the artist he has the problem of creating something that is not the exact duplicate of some previous creation. (LW 9: 198)

Artistic gardeners and metalworkers—as well as artistic teachers—rely on standards and judgments that have been established and made in the past after a careful analysis of relevant considerations: the seeds, the ores; the generals, the particulars; the environments, the treatments; the boundaries, the poten-tialities. But no true artist stops with these extremely valuable considerations.

Instead, she asks, "What can I contribute to the process of enabling this person to become uniquely and desirably different? What conditions, suggestions, and directions can I provide that will facilitate her personal growth?"

When answering these questions, the teacher's originality and inventiveness leads her to pursue tested and experimental educational opportunities with each student. No matter how excellent prior students and classes have been, she focuses on present students. No matter how compelled she feels to shape a student into a prior masterpiece, she doesn't settle for reproducing previous successes. Fortunately, she uses the uniqueness of each student to lead this aspiration. Together they—teacher and student—collaborate to construct an independently choosing and thinking person.

As you reflect on the implication of cultivating the rich diversity we find in students, think for a moment about what you believe may be the great temptations of teachers, the enticements that may pull us away from the ideal? Is one temptation that of allowing or even encouraging students to focus on satisfying us rather than on their learning to think independently (LW 8: 160–161)? And what factors do you think may help us decide not to yield to these temptations?

A SUMMATIVE EXERCISE

Chapter 6   The Teacher as Gardener

Understandings	Qualities	Activities

READINGS

"Aims in Education," in *Democracy and Education* (MW 9: 107–117).
"Education as Growth," in *Democracy and Education* (MW 9: 46–58).
"The Need for a Philosophy of Education," (LW 9: 194–204).
"Progressive Organization of Subject-Matter," in *Experience and Education* (LW 113: 48–60).

NOTE

1. An example of how Dewey's thought may have been practiced on a wide scale is found in the segregated African American schools in the southern United States during the early and middle parts of the 20th century. Many African American educators were well acquainted with his thought and used his ideas in culturally and imaginatively important ways. See Vanessa Siddle Walker's *Their Highest Potential* (University of North Carolina Press, 1996).

SEVEN

The Teacher as Educational Pioneer

What they [inventive educational pioneers] need above all else is the creatively courageous disposition. Fear, routine, sloth, identification of success with ease, and approbation of others are the enemies that now stand in the way of educational advance. Too much of what is called educational science and art only perpetuate a regime of wont and use by pretending to give scientific guidance and guarantees in advance. There is in existence knowledge which gives a compass to those who enter on the uncharted seas, but only a stupid insincerity will claim that a compass is a chart. The call is to the creative adventurous mind. Religious faith in education working through this medium of individual courage with the aid of non-educational science will end in achieving education as a science and art. But as usual we confuse faith with worship, and term science what is only justification of habit.

—John Dewey (MW 13: 328)

Authors' Note: References to works by John Dewey are from the collection of his works published by Southern Illinois University Press: *The Early Works of John Dewey, 1882–1898; The Middle Works of John Dewey, 1899–1924;* and *The Later Works of John Dewey, 1925–1953.* References to these works are abbreviated as EW, MW, and LW, where, for example, EW 5: 94 indicates that the material cited or idea noted is in *The Early Works,* Volume 5, page 94.

I n this remark, we find Dewey thinking about several pertinent issues for
the teacher. Among them is his concern for what we might call educational
or school reform and what he terms "radical renovation of the school system"
(MW 13: 323). In "Education as Engineering" (1922), he appears angry as he
thinks through some similarities between engineering and education, especially building bridges and building schools. His rather dogmatic conclusions
may surprise us: that we need teachers who are governed not by traditions,
conventions, fears, habits, complacency, docility, and laziness but by coura-
geousness, imagination, assertiveness, experimentation, creativity, and adventurousness. Dewey believes that if we develop a new attitude toward teaching
that is characterized by the second set of qualities and dispositions, we can
develop an art of teaching or "art of educational engineering" (MW 13: 325).
Until we abandon the former set and choose the latter, he claims that there can
be no art of education.

Let's push a little farther to see how he arrives at his conclusions and to
determine what his thinking means for us, especially for positive changes in
teaching, learning, and schooling. What ideas are influencing Dewey's comments at this time? Six or seven distinct thoughts seem to emerge. First, he
believes that school systems are dominated by traditions and are not adequately influenced by experimentation and application of the recently
learned. Little thinking occurs, so we get the same educational results.
Second, he thinks that educational theory has produced new ideas of schooling and teaching that reach far beyond what is generally allowed in schools.
Credible educational theory exists, but it matters little if there isn't freedom
for and interest in its implementation. Third, he argues that there is a growing body of knowledge about education that is not being appropriately
applied. New findings have emerged about teaching and learning, but old
practices still dominate schools. Fourth, he fears that many educators are too
concerned with finding sets of information (rather than a body of knowledge) that yield explicit, detailed directions for how to teach each child.
Educators' inappropriate expectations mean that findings that require reflection fade away or remain unapplied. Fifth, he feels that too many people
expect a science of education to emerge before there has been sufficient
experimentation. Where there is little experimentation, we can expect a
stagnant, underdeveloped science of education. More experimentation and
research are needed. Sixth, he says that too much research focuses on
improving existing practices and traditions, not on creating a new kind of

education. Studying existing practices, therefore, ensures that we will not have new practices, much less a different kind of education and schooling. Finally, he reasons that much, perhaps most, of what is considered change in schools is a recycling of the familiar in new verbal garb or under the label of a novel name. The new, at least in many cases, is little more than the old with a novel wrapper.

Does this sound familiar or ring true? Yes, too much of it does. Is this where Dewey leaves us, with a criticism that provides no guidance about where we can think about going? Does he suggest a means of liberating ourselves from these traditions, trends, and tendencies? Are there grounds for being hopeful?

His answer is relatively straightforward. We need to use our minds, imagination, and reflection as we experiment with different ways of educating. As we use our minds, we need to transform them to think "out of line with convention and custom" (MW 13: 325). This suggestion sounds much like "thinking outside the box." Whatever the similarities, we don't need to exchange one box, set of lines, or dogma for another one. Nor do we need to concentrate on just evaluating and criticizing the lines and boxes of others. We have our own habits, traditions, conventions, and customs that enclose and restrict our intellectual movements no matter how liberated we think we are. They become apparent—at least to others—nearly every time we discuss a different way of thinking about an issue, solving a problem, testing an idea, or rearranging educational variables. So, let's aim our criticisms at our own hedges first and the enclosures of others second, or at least evaluate them simultaneously.

As we use our minds to get outside of their—better, *our*—inhibiting barriers, Dewey says that we will create new minds, minds that are guided by experimentation and reflection. As we use our imagination, we look for opportunities to apply, implement, and experiment with the new theories and research that have reached beyond existing practices. As we use our abilities to reflect on what we are learning in the process of experimentation—our successes and failures—we need to be honest with ourselves so that we can develop suggestions for an intelligent educational art, the recreation of teaching and schools, and the facilitation of the growth of students.

But Dewey knows that thinking, using our imaginations, and experimenting are not easy. Our environments, beliefs, values, and dispositions

> **A Teacher Snapshot**
>
> Sketch a composite picture of the courageous teachers you have met.
>
> What other attributes of an artistic teacher did they possess? Did their courage ever work against them?
>
> Can you pick out differences of situation and personality that complemented or hindered these teachers' success?

are significant forces in keeping our schools and us as we are. Yet we shouldn't change too easily, because it takes time to think things through, digest new ideas and research, and evaluate new theories. But there is another factor that makes thinking and changing difficult: fear. Fundamentally, we are too afraid to change much. Fear, intimidation, and timidity are our great enemies.

Given this perspective, how can we change? Dewey is lucid when responding to this question: We must be courageous. In fact, he uses the words *courageous* or *courage* seven times in his very brief article to underline the importance of the concept.

His comments raise a question: How do intimidated and timid people, if that is what we are, become courageous? Dewey does not give us an explicit answer to this question, but we can think and discover some answers for ourselves. Seeking answers, we can actually begin with his indirect comments on the subject and start building another kind of culture that promotes courageously acting teachers. The answer regarding how to build a new culture rests in part on attracting and retaining greater numbers of teachers who are not inclined to be docile. Likewise, it may rest in part on recruiting and keeping more teachers who are experimentally inclined. Of course, it will be helpful to attract, encourage, and retain administrators who understand the deadly effect of routine and mindlessness in teaching and schools. Maybe we should even encourage some of the courageous but equally creative, reflective, caring, flexible, and fair-minded teachers we know to become administrators—and remind them not to become transformed into bureaucrats by the people and problems they encounter. We want people who are cultural transformers, not conformers, to enter the field of administration.

Dewey's indirect comments go beyond these suggestions, however. He speaks of the courage to think imaginatively, but thinking creatively isn't the same as behaving differently. It may be a step in that direction, however. Informally

Table 7.1   The Friends and Enemies of the Educational Pioneer

The Friends	The Enemies
Courage	Fear
Variety	Repetition
Imagination	Commonplace
Assertiveness	Docility
Creativity	Routine ✓
Inventiveness	Laziness
Adventurousness	Timidity
Experimentation	Tradition
Reflection	Absorption
Science	Habit✓
Faith	Doubt

encouraging and practicing imaginative thinking may be a small step, but it seems better than no step at all. But even being creative, to a degree, is permissible in most contexts. So thinking (to a large degree) and teaching (at least to a small degree) creatively is probably something that is doable for the overwhelming majority of us. We can start with our own mind, move out into our particular classroom, and, when we collaborate with likeminded colleagues, extend ourselves down the halls into other classrooms. As thinkers and infiltrators working on behalf of imagination, we can change more than we may initially believe.

We can easily conclude that the friends and enemies of the teaching pioneer are many. Ideally, we will align ourselves with the friends of the artistic spirit and seek to diminish the influence of those who for numerous reasons resist discovering new and better ways of educating children and youth. Table 7.1 reminds us that we need to select our friends or, rather, colleagues carefully, for we need teachers around us who are characterized by the qualities of friends, not enemies.

More is involved if Dewey is correct. He implies—or at least we infer—that a strong faith in education will actively work in us to nurture the courage to do what is in the best interest of children and youth. A few of us have never had faith that educators and schooling can make a major difference in individuals and society. Perhaps others of us have a weak or nearly dead faith. Still others of us may have buried our faith years ago in a pedagogical cemetery with little fanfare and the epitaph, "Here Lies My Hope for Schools, Teachers, and Students." Or maybe we cremated our deceased faith and had the ashes scattered over the world's schoolyards. If we are accurately described by any of these scenarios, we no doubt need to explore ways to revitalize ourselves. Without a personal vitality and passion for what we do, we are almost certain to lack an imaginative and pioneering spirit and an artistically and aesthetically appealing classroom. With a moral conviction that schools should serve children and youth well, we can have hope of reigniting our faith in the power of learning and thinking and the teaching that enhances both.

Feeling alone is seldom a good thing. We should recognize, therefore, that we are not alone in our desires, for we can count on the help of existing courageous teachers. Some of us probably had the way paved for us by others, for there are courageous and imaginative teachers and administrators sprinkled in districts nearly everywhere. Some of us, in fact, are so confident and spirited that we open doors for others to be creative, experimental, and reflective. Even the "harmless eccentric" can help create latitude for us to be artistic and experimental in our teaching.

In essence, we are well advised to look within as well as around us as we look for conditions and people that will enable us to overcome and go around traditions, fears, habits, docility, and laziness to develop our courage, imagination, assertiveness, experimentation, and adventurousness. As we replace the dominance of the former with the predominance of the latter, we will see a cultural shift that returns art to schooling and teaching and, we hope, contributes to that art of education that is so badly needed.

QUOTES AND QUESTIONS

We haven't mentioned Dewey's book *Art as Experience* in the last several chapters. Hence, let's return to an important idea about the nature of the artist:

> One of the essential traits of the artist is that he is born an experimenter. Without this trait he becomes a poor or a good academician. The artist is compelled to be an experimenter because he has to express an intensely individualized experience through means and materials that belong to the common and public world. This problem cannot be solved once for all. It is met in every new work undertaken. Otherwise an artist repeats himself and becomes esthetically dead. Only because the artist operates experimentally does he open new fields of experience and disclose new aspects and qualities in familiar scenes and objects. (LW 10: 148–149)

Being an experimenter is one of the essential traits, he says. He doesn't hedge by saying desirable, admirable, important, key, or principal characteristics.

Of course, he would probably say experimentation is all of these things, but the more important idea is that the artist is an experimenter. To not experiment is to declare that one is a nonartist? Can you think of a sound argument against Dewey's assertion? Are most of the options he allows as follows: Artists never experiment, artists seldom experiment, artists frequently experiment, artists nearly always experiment, and artists always experiment? Which of these options do you think is the better one overall? Or do you have a more appropriate suggestion or viewpoint?

What do you think of the word *born* in the first sentence of the previous quote? Does the fact that Dewey says we are all born with instincts toward the communicative, constructive, inquisitive, and artistic illuminate the subject (MW 1: 30)? In what ways, then, are we all born artists or with artistic potentialities?

Let's change the subject: Should we be satisfied with a teacher who is just a good academician? Is she likely to have the loves we discussed regarding a successful teacher? Or will she become in time like the pedant that Dewey describes in his poem "To a Pedant"?

> Could we peep within thy mind
> 'Tis sure that we should find
> Store rooms clean swept and garnisht
> With ornaments deckt out for show;
> In its middle, marble hall—
> Sharp cut mosaics on its wall—
> With paved pool long since outfished
> Of any living things that grow.
>
> —Boydston, 1977, p. 78

Perhaps we can think of other options that Dewey should have mentioned. If you think there are other options, which do you think is the most viable one?

IMPLICATIONS FOR THE TEACHER

What do we learn in this instance about Dewey's view of the art of teaching? Among other things, we learn that he associates the science of teaching with the art of teaching. In fact, science contributes knowledge that informs artistic teaching (LW 3: 268) and is "the intelligent factor *in* art," or the means of accomplishing the end toward which art works (LW 1: 276). It is this scientific understanding, including the ability to reflect on and evaluate it, which informs art that partially enables the teacher to be successful in "the most difficult and the most important of all human arts" (LW 3: 268). If we want to be artists, then, we need to understand, think with, and act on the warranted scientific studies that inform teaching, learning, and educational administration. But we retain the wisdom of a mother and discretion of a judge. Being mindless about research, data, and theory is not an option for the artist.

> **A Reflective Opportunity**
>
> If Dewey is correct, does our ability to practice the art of teaching depend in part on our understanding of the science of education or educational theory?

If you read "Education as Engineering," you ran across such terms as *reflect, new, creative, inventive, adventurous, experiment, pioneer,* and *imaginative* and learned that these words are often associated with the idea of art. Likewise, you learned that other words are frequently associated with stymieing original thought and artistic practice, such as *fear, custom, habit, bondage, routine, timidity, docility, old,* and *laziness.* But Dewey cautions that merely changing our terms or vocabulary will not change schools, teaching, and learning. He insists that

> new conceptions in education will not of themselves carry us far in modifying schools, for until the schools are modified the new conceptions will be themselves pale, remote, vague, formal. They will become thick, substantial, only in the degree in which they are not indispensably required. For they offer precise and definite modes of thinking only when new meanings and values have become embodied in concrete life-experiences and are thus sustained by them. Till that time arrives the importance of new concepts is mainly negative and critical. They enable us to criticize existing modes of practice; they point out to us the fact that concrete detail of the right sort does *not* exist. Their positive function is to inspire experimental action rather than to give information as to how to execute it. (MW 13: 324)

How, then, can the teacher use language in such a way that she facilitates critical analysis and inspires experimental action? The former activity—critical analysis—without the latter often appears to result in an environment that is devoid of both professional pleasure and purpose. What steps can we take to ensure that our new beliefs and terms become integrated into teaching and broader school activities?

We opened this section with a question: What do we learn in this instance about Dewey's view of the art of teaching? As we end it, we ask: What have we learned about ourselves and the possibility of being an educational pioneer in the future? Do we have the courage to work with other teachers on experimental reading or math programs? What new materials and methods have we used this year? Do we take the time to imagine different ways of teaching students who are not grasping particular ideas or learning specific skills? When told we cannot try a new approach, do we quietly go away or stay to argue for our beliefs? Do we speak up to defend colleagues when they are criticized for creating alternative ways of teaching or learning? When was the last time we used some recent research to change classroom arrangements, methods, or assignments? Do we really reflect on or study what we do as educators? Have we identified any useful patterns or insights in the last year or so? Do we believe that we can make a difference in the life of a student or school? Are we growing in educational artistry? On the other hand, do we see ourselves or do others see us as living with the enemies of pioneer educational work? Do the commonplace, fear, repetition, docility, routine, laziness, timidity, tradition, absorption, habit, and doubt make us merely educational employees? Do we like what we have learned about ourselves?

A SUMMATIVE EXERCISE

Chapter 7   The Teacher as Educational Pioneer

Understandings	Qualities	Activities

READINGS

"Dewey Outlines Utopian Schools," (LW 9: 136–140).

"Education as Engineering," (MW 13: 323–328).

"Monastery, Bargain Counter, or Laboratory in Education?" (LW 6: 99–111).

"To a Pedant." (1977). In J. A. Boydston (Ed.), *The Poems of John Dewey* (p. 78). Carbondale: Southern Illinois University.

EIGHT

The Teacher
as Servant

So I appeal to teachers in the face of every hysterical wave of emotion, and of every subtle appeal of sinister class interest, to remember that they above all others are the consecrated servants of democratic ideas in which alone this country is truly a distinctive nation—ideas of friendly and helpful intercourse between all and the equipment of every individual to serve the community by his own best powers in his own best way.

—John Dewey (MW 10: 210)

E arlier, we mentioned that Dewey believes students need to develop a view of life that helps them get beyond personal interests to consider the interests of others, including the people in their schools, communities, nation, and world. We argued that their developed abilities, perceptions, and sensitivities should be adapted to meet the needs of society, including promoting a culture that takes into consideration the importance of living democratically, which means much more than just voting for political candidates. Likewise,

---

Authors' Note: References to works by John Dewey are from the collection of his works published by Southern Illinois University Press: *The Early Works of John Dewey, 1882–1898; The Middle Works of John Dewey, 1899–1924;* and *The Later Works of John Dewey, 1925–1953.* References to these works are abbreviated as EW, MW, and LW, where, for example, EW 5: 94 indicates that the material cited or idea noted is in *The Early Works,* Volume 5, page 94.

we observed that doing chemistry, history, biology, art, physics, and music are socially important activities and should be learned with more than individual development and career ambitions in mind. This idea, of course, is not new to anyone who has studied Dewey, for his basic idea—that we as teachers need a commitment to building, expanding, sustaining, and refining a democratic society—is stated in capsule form in his "My Pedagogic Creed":

> I believe, finally, that the teacher is engaged, not simply in the training of individuals, but in the formation of the proper social life. I believe that every teacher should realize the dignity of his calling; that he is a social servant set apart for the maintenance of proper social order and the securing of the right social growth. I believe that in this way the teacher always is the prophet of the true God and the usherer in of the true kingdom of God. (EW 5: 95)

But his democratic ideas and ideals go much farther. In fact, his magnum opus—*Democracy and Education*—explores the relationship between democracy and education in some detail, as do many of his essays. In one essay, "Nationalizing Education" (1916), he examines the causes of war, a "go-as-you-please" individualism, and a narrow form of nationalism that he thinks are antithetical to democracy. Pointedly, he objects to, among other things, "a local, provincial, sectarian and partisan spirit" that promotes its own interests and slights the interests of other classes, races, and cultures (MW 10: 203). His view of living democratically, then, argues against much of what goes on in many societies, especially in times of national and world crises. This means, as far as he is concerned, that schools have a delicate and challenging role to play in being counter-culture during times that antidemocratic tendencies are most pronounced. If they are silent, they may be viewed as a cause of undemocratic lifestyles, policies, and practices. What role, however, can the teacher—and groups of teachers and schools—play in promoting democracy when so many forces work in undemocratic ways for partisan goals? Recognizing that schools occupy a precarious position and cannot often depart significantly from social and political leadership, Dewey suggests that we can regularly and consistently promote a series of values that will help nurture an ongoing democratic ethos:

- the will to cooperate with others,
- the right of everyone to share in cultural and material resources,
- the desirability of a just and humanitarian society,
- the advantages of a common understanding, and
- the importance of mutual compassion and benevolence (LW 9: 203–204).

Table 8.1   Two Kinds of Nationalism

Negative Nationalism	*Positive Nationalism*
Unity within by nurturing dislike for those without	Unity of feeling and aim for those within and without
Separation of peoples	Freedom of intercourse by peoples
Foe of internationalism	Friend of internationalism
Fear of those who are different	Respect for diverse people
Preparation for war	Promotion of peace
Lack of trust in schools to cultivate unity	Faith in schools to cultivate ideas, emotions, dispositions, and outlooks

Nurturing these values before, during, and after national and international crises serves society well.

He makes other suggestions, however. For example, he pushes for democratic living and teaching that is allied with what he views as a positive nationalism, not a negative or counterproductive one. A few of the negative and the positive qualities he identifies are contrasted in Table 8.1.

Dewey's answers, however, move beyond the roles schools and teachers have in promoting positive nationalism and complementary democratic ideals to the issue of accountability (MW 10: 203–207). He contends that the chief form of accountability for a school system is found in the answer to a single question. That is, the question of accountability is tied to what the

> public school [has] done toward subordinating a local, provincial, sectarian and partisan spirit of mind to aims and interests which are common to all men and women of the country—to what extent has it taught men [and women] to think and feel in ideas broad enough to be inclusive of the purposes and happiness of all sections and classes? (MW 10: 203)

The accountability factors that he identifies overlap, of course, with his previously mentioned values, but he adds a specific concern for gender, social, and economic groups and classes. His next words sound ominous:

> For unless the agencies which form the mind and morals of the community can prevent the operation of those forces which are always making for a division of interests, class and sectional ideas and feelings will become dominant, and our democracy will fall to pieces. (MW 10: 203)

The ethical criterion that he focuses on is whether schools undermine tendencies that divide people and promote a concern for common welfare.

Fortunately, the school is only one of "the agencies" that should be involved in promoting democracy (MW 10: 203). But Dewey sometimes attributes to it an enormous power and influence for assisting in the development of a positive nationalism. In fact, he describes democracy as if it has a life cycle and the role of education as that of midwife: "Democracy has to be born anew every generation, and education is its midwife" (MW 10: 139). The teacher, as a "nurse of democracy" (LW 11: 416), works with other teachers, and the school works with other educational agencies to bring forth new generations of democratically thinking and acting individuals. Although other agencies should promote a positive nationalism, let's return to the role of teachers and schools in promoting democratic ideals. What are our duties as midwives, nurses, and servants of democratic ideas? In essence, it seems we are responsible for helping form both the mind and morals of students. Here, we may back away from Dewey, for we recognize that moral education is controversial. In fact, some believe that schools should not form students in any way, including guiding the development of

> ### A Teacher Snapshot
>
> Do you recall a teacher who served as a midwife or nurse for democratic values? Was she widely known for her values, ideas, or techniques? Or all three? Create a rich snapshot of her so that she is more than a promoter of values.

the mind. Others think forming morals is wrong or, at least, too risky and, therefore, should be avoided by teachers and schools. Still others, including Dewey, do not agree with our rejecting the forming of minds or the forming of morals. Why, someone may wonder, would such a reflective person as Dewey subscribe to such an unsound point of view? Because bright people are not necessarily correct on all issues? Perhaps. Because he is a covert cultural imperialist? Maybe. Because he doesn't understand that he is subtly introducing his white, middle-class, male values into schools? Possibly. Because he doesn't understand that he's attempting to impose his morals on children? Not really. He actually writes a great deal about imposition and understands it is unethical.

These questions deserve careful exploration, as do many related queries. But they would take us too far afield if we pursued them now. So, we will return to Dewey's ideas and a very brief statement about why he thinks we should form both minds and morals. First, he thinks we abandon our moral responsibilities as adults and educators if we leave the formation of the mind and morals to nature, chance, or culture. Second, he argues that education as education is a moral endeavor and cannot be otherwise; it is permeated with moral choices and activities. Third, he believes that the promotion of democratic ideals is a moral and intellectual undertaking. For instance, the previously mentioned democratic ideals—the will to cooperate with others, the right of everyone to share in cultural and material resources, the desirability of a just and humanitarian society, the advantages of a common understanding, and the importance of mutual compassion and

---

A Reflective Opportunity

If someone wishes to be ethically or morally neutral in the classroom and school, is that possible? If it is, is neutrality itself an ethical issue? Is it a conclusion that is similar to deciding to be a pacifist?

---

benevolence—are intellectual, moral, and democratic values. These thoughts, however, do not tell us all we want to know about moral education or how he thinks it or character development should proceed. We merely note that it should proceed largely in an "indirect, slow, gradual, and unconscious" manner (MW 6: 388). But, if so, is this process education or socialization? His answer is worth pursuing.

Now, let's attempt again to look at what teachers and schools ought to do to promote democratic ideals and, if Dewey is correct, moral education or character development. When pursuing our responsibilities in the promotion of democratic living, he says schools and teachers have a twofold task: (1) to promote the growth of specific qualities and (2) to discourage the development of other characteristics. The former set of characteristics includes such characteristics as respect, friendliness, kindness, tolerance, forbearance, well-wishing, and amity. The latter set involves fear, suspicion, jealousy, hatred, distrust, and enmity. Dewey asks us if we are committed to encouraging democracy and, thereby, cultivating the former and uprooting the latter. Or are we attempting the impossible: to be neutral in our dealings with moral or ethical issues? Do we really think that being neutral on issues of respect, fairness, and freedom is well-advised if it is even possible, much less ethical? Unlike Dewey, do we wish to say that neither schools nor teachers are the midwives or nurses of democracy?

The school's moral accountability can be assessed in other ways, too. For example, Dewey asks if we as teachers are distressed about the circumstances of the "oppressed," "unfortunate," and "disinherited," or do we find ourselves silent about circumstances and issues that leave intact or worsen the circumstances for these individuals and groups (MW 10: 207–208)? Moreover, are we making our schools "energetic and willing instrument[s] in developing initiative, courage, power, and personal ability in each individual" and, thereby, achieving "equal opportunity for all" (MW 10: 209)? Do we, furthermore, actively engage in promoting "the common struggle of native born, African, Jew, Italian and . . . a score of other peoples" to attain freedom and education (MW 10: 206)? Are we attempting to equalize opportunity by helping the majority of people overcome the "accidental inequalities of birth, wealth, and learning" that come with the resources of inherited wealth (MW 10: 138)? In short, are we servants of democratic ideals?

Explicitly, it is obvious that Dewey promotes democratic societies. Implicitly, it is clear that he is interested in a multicultural democracy.[1] In fact, he goes beyond implicit statements. He openly argues that the nationalism of the United States is "complex and compound" and "interracial and international" (MW 10: 204). Anyone who fails to appreciate this diversity, he claims, is a "traitor" to the genuine nationalism that exists in the country (MW 10: 204). In promoting what he calls "real nationalism," he recommends enriching larger cultural patterns in the country by "drawing out and composing into a harmonious whole the best, the most characteristic" features of each culture, race, and group (MW 10: 204). A nation will be more attractive and stronger, he believes, if the best of all groups is contributed to the whole rather than isolated and privately held in smaller groups. But he adamantly opposes a homogeneous society or a conformity that is based on one group's race or culture (MW 10: 204). In the broader, cultural "harmonious whole," no one group can "do anything but furnish one note in a vast symphony." But each contributes to "a common fund of wisdom and experience" (MW 10: 205).[2] Dangers, nevertheless, exist for groups in a diverse nation, for example, physical isolation, cultural autogamy, educational imposition, social stagnation, and inauthentic nationalism. Specifically, he avers:

> The dangerous thing is for each factor to isolate itself, to try to live off its past, and then to attempt to impose itself upon other elements, or at least, to keep itself intact and thus refuse to accept what other cultures have to offer, so as to thereby to be transmuted into authentic Americanism. (MW 10: 205)

The challenge to build an authentic nation is one of changing the intellectual, emotional, and moral perspectives and dispositions of people by means of educational agencies, particularly public schools (MW 10: 203). Specifically, the school needs to teach each segment of society to respect everyone and understand the mutual contributions of one another. Moreover, it is important to teach that hyphenates—for example, African-American, Irish-American, Mexican-American, German-American, Korean-American, English-American, Jewish-American, Scottish-American, Chinese-American— connect us rather than separate us. Each of us *is* American (MW 10: 205). Beyond these emphases, Dewey claims that schools ought to pay more attention in the formal curriculum to "the great waves" of immigration into a country, make each student aware of "the rich breadth" of a nation's composition, and help each person realize "the peculiarity of *our* nationalism is its internationalism" (MW 10: 206). By consciously undertaking these responsibilities, teachers become "pioneers in improving the welfare of the mass of the people" (MW 15: 156). "Teaching," consequently, is "an adventure on the social frontier" where advances are to be made in advancing democratic practices and living, and "the classroom is a kind of test-tube for social living" (LW 11: 547, 541).

With these views of democracy, diversity, character development, and education, we do not need to speculate about why Dewey refers to teachers as "the consecrated servants of democratic ideas" nor why he claims that

> the business of the educator—whether parent or teacher—is to see to it that the greatest possible number of ideas acquired by children and youth are acquired in such a vital way that they become *moving* ideas, motive-forces in the guidance of conduct. This demand and this opportunity make the moral purpose universal and dominant in all instruction—whatsoever the topic. Were it not for this possibility, the familiar statement that the ultimate purpose of all education is character-forming would be hypocritical pretense; for as everyone knows, the direct and immediate attention of teachers and pupils must be, for the greater part of time, upon intellectual matters. It is out of the question to keep direct moral considerations constantly uppermost. But it is not out of the question to aim at making the methods of learning, of acquiring intellectual power, and of assimilating subject-matter, such that they will render behavior more enlightened, more consistent, more vigorous than it otherwise would be. (MW 4: 267–268)

QUOTES AND QUESTIONS

Dewey makes an interesting, perhaps startling, assertion about the social and personal function of art when he says:

> Just as it is the office of art to be unifying, to break through conventional distinctions to the underlying common elements of the experienced world, while developing individuality as the manner of seeing and expressing these elements, so it is the office of art in the individual person, to compose differences, to do away with isolations and conflicts among elements of our being, to utilize oppositions among them to build a richer personality. (LW 10: 252–253)

What shall we make of this declaration? Is he correct when he maintains that art serves to develop individuality in human perception and unity in human reception both socially and individually? Do we really develop more integrated and richer personalities and a more unified society by having the arts in our lives? If so, then "all art is a process of making the world a different place in which to live" (LW 1: 272). These ideas lead, if we think they are reasonably sound, to asking whether art in the curriculum and art in pedagogy lead to "a remaking of the experience of the community [and a community of learners] in the direction of greater order and unity" (LW 10: 87). Another way of thinking about this question is to ask if there is moral, character, and perceptual development potential in the arts for individuals and society. Furthermore, we may wish to ask: If Dewey's beliefs about art having a positive effect on individuals and society are warranted, do they imply that artistic teaching has a similar influence on individual students and classes of students?

IMPLICATIONS FOR THE TEACHER

As we look at the implications of the ideas in this chapter for the teacher, thinking about a few questions may serve us well. First, do we know of any empirical studies that support or discredit Dewey's claims? That is, are we aware of any well-developed studies about the effect of art on social and personal development? Second, if the answer to the first question confirms in part or in whole Dewey's claim, do we have an obligation to give more attention to the arts curricula in schools? And do we have a more compelling justification to refine our art of teaching if he is correct on this particular point? Third, if Dewey's claims about the positive influence of art are incorrect, poorly substantiated, or neglected by researchers, are we still obligated to become the social servants he claims? If yes, what more do we need to learn to do our jobs with increasing success?

Let's also examine how Dewey's ideas about democracy may influence our classrooms and schools. To start, we should remind ourselves that classrooms and schools should be democratic learning communities. Initially, we may think that this idea is nonsense if we have been led to believe that the essence of democracy is majority rule. Dewey agrees and doesn't suggest that students should vote on whether they want a teacher, a principal, a board, or a curriculum. This point is somewhat similar to saying that a political democracy doesn't allow us to vote on whether we want to have a prime minister or president, a parliament or congress, or a charter or constitution. Likewise, Dewey is opposed to any so-called democracy that does not protect the rights of minorities. Their rights cannot be set aside by a majority vote. In addition to these negative implications of democracy, Dewey refers to some positive implications of democracy and a democratically oriented classroom and school. His thoughts are rooted in his threefold interpretation of democracy as a (1) "form of government" (LW 11: 236), (2) "way of associated living" (LW 13: 155), and (3) *personal way of individual life*" (LW 14: 226). The overlap among these three realms is obvious, both for society and for school.

> ### An Introspective Moment
>
> In what ways do you think you are a servant of democratic ideas? Would you like to add anything to your activities in this realm? rethink anything?

Looking at school and classroom implications of democracy as a form of government may be the best place to begin our discussion. As a student learns about and experiences democracy as a form of government, Dewey expects citizenship education to include developing each student so that she has

- the capacity to vote intelligently,
- the disposition to comply with ethical laws,
- the competence to contribute economically to society,
- the knowledge to function thoughtfully as a member of a family,
- the ability to think independently,
- the capability to serve sympathetically as a member of society, and
- the aptitude to lead democratically (MW 4: 269ff).

A key consideration for teachers is to determine how we will help lead schools and design our classrooms to reflect on and nurture these capacities. Questions, of course, abound. What can we do to ensure that every student gets involved in democratic leadership opportunities? How do we get students involved in serving one another and the community? Is it an outdated idea to think that students should learn to function as members of a family? What exactly does that mean? Dare we discuss when it might be appropriate to disobey a law, even an unethical one? What does it mean to comply with ethical laws?

Next, let's look at a few of the ideas Dewey attaches to the concept of democracy as a way of associated living. Being aware that a democratic government is a shallow if crucial victory apart from an environment that facilitates and supports social justice, basic freedoms, individual respect, and personal safety, Dewey pushes his ideals outside official government matters into communities and, eventually, schools. He argues that our communities and schools need to promote

> a way of life controlled by a working faith in the possibilities of human nature. Belief in the Common Man [and Woman] is a familiar article in the democratic creed. That belief is without basis and significance save as it means faith in the potentialities of human nature as that nature is exhibited in every human being irrespective of race, color, sex, birth and family, of material or cultural wealth. This faith may be enacted in statutes, but it is only on paper unless it is put in force in the attitudes which human beings display to one another in all the incidents and relations of daily life. (LW 14: 226)

The implications of democracy for daily life include among other ideals, the practice of nurturing in students

- the tendency to encourage equal opportunity for the development of everyone;
- the predisposition to support freedom of lifestyle for everyone;
- the inclination to promote open communication among like- and unlike-minded peoples;
- the bent to develop cooperative activities for the common good;
- the disposition to seek resolution of disagreements by discussions and interactions;
- the willingness to work toward the basic needs of each person;
- the penchant to consider the interests and aspirations of everyone; and
- the proclivity to support the growth of common and personal interests. (LW 14: 226–228; MW 9: 7–9)

Needless to say, educators have many opportunities to cultivate these sometimes tangled and conflicting dispositions. For example, how do we facilitate student interactions about allowing people to choose their own lifestyles and, at the same time, work toward the common good? When does open communication become a hindrance to rather than a help to addressing differences of opinion? What role does ongoing education have for associated living? When, if ever, do we set aside personal aspirations for the good of society as a whole?

Finally, we need to examine democracy as a personal way of life. Dewey adds this theme or, perhaps, subtheme to associated living, to avoid an important misunderstanding. That is, he wants to clarify that government laws and social life are extremely important but inadequate if the individual remains unchanged in her attitudes, feelings, and thinking. Democracy is founded at least in part on internal and personal attitudes, not merely external laws and mores. Consequently, he argues that schools and teachers should be interested in a moral education that goes beyond citizenship education and community interaction and ought to cultivate on the part of students:

- the attitudes that advance a personal practice of democratic values even when the legal backdrop and social environment are unsupportive;
- the character that enables a person to choose democratic ideals over personal privilege and social esteem;
- the habits that incline a person to promote democratic living in everyday activities and choices; and
- the faith that enables a person to adhere to democratic means of freedom, education, and discussion over authoritarian and dictatorial means to achieve democratic goals. (LW 14: 226–230)

As teachers, we will want to explore how we can and should foster these attitudes, character, habits, and faith without being unethical and while being critical. We might even ask ourselves and our students if Dewey is overly committed to democracy—as a form of government, a way of living, and a personal lifestyle. Is his faith worth the risks that it appears to foster? Alternatively, is his faith dated? If so, how might we want to update it?

Considering these few ideas—democracy as a form of government, as an associated way of existence, and as personal living—makes it obvious why Dewey thinks that education is the midwife of democracy and why the art of teaching is a crucial element in being an effective servant of democratic ideals. Our practicing democracy in time becomes an actual part of our art of teaching and, ideally, a part of the political, social, and personal fabric of a country.

A SUMMATIVE EXERCISE

Chapter 8   The Teacher as Servant

Understandings	Qualities	Activities

READINGS

"Character," (MW 6: 381–388).
"Creative Democracy—The Task Before Us," (LW 14: 224–230).
"Education and Social Change," (LW 11: 408–417).
"Education as a Social Function," in *Democracy and Education* (MW 9: 14–27).
Moral Principles in Education (MW 4: 265–291).
"Nationalizing Education," (MW 10: 202–210).

NOTES

1. Dewey does not employ the term *multiculturalism*, but some of his emphases are parallel to its present-day values.

2. The fact that Dewey says each group should "surrender" the best of its culture or "its special good" to help "create the national spirit of America" is not one the

authors share if he means that the contributing group no longer possesses that special good (MW 10: 205). To us—and probably Dewey—such surrender makes no sense. Why completely give away your best cultural features? If a group completely surrenders or gives away its "best, most characteristic" qualities and "special good[s]" for the health of a broader culture, it may help the greater good but only at the expense of the cultural impoverishment and, possibly, death of the smaller group. Dewey doesn't favor the death of contributing cultures, for they are valuable entities and contribute to the vitality and health of the larger culture. Conversely, if he means that we should share—offer up for others to learn from and enjoy—our particular culture's riches with one another so that we can appreciate and adopt whatever we wish, that is another matter. His use of the word *contributions* of a culture to another supports this latter interpretation (MW 10: 205). His use of *surrender* in other contexts supports this latter interpretation, too. The term is used in several ways, including implying that when one surrenders knowledge or values to others, the giver or givers are no longer the sole possessors of the truth or value. Everyone, including the giver or givers, can be possessors. His explanation of art and conversation is similar:

> In a work of art, different acts, episodes, occurrences melt and fuse into unity, and yet do not disappear and lose their own character as they do so—just as in a genial conversation there is a continuous interchange and blending, and yet each speaker not only retains his own character but manifests it more clearly than is his wont. (LW 10: 43–44)

NINE

The Teacher as Social Engineer

We may fairly enough call educational practice a kind of social engineering.

—John Dewey (LW 5: 20)

W e examined Dewey's conception of the teacher as an educational pioneer earlier. In that context, Dewey speaks of the physical and constructive engineer and stresses that constructive engineers who were pioneers used their knowledge and imagination to experiment with building different types of bridges that were more suitable for the age. He remarks that when engineers first attempted to imagine a new kind of bridge, the imagination of nearly everyone was "held in bondage by habituation to what was already familiar" (MW 13: 325). We, as educators, he thinks, are in many ways like most engineers in that patterns of thought about what schools

Authors' Note: References to works by John Dewey are from the collection of his works published by Southern Illinois University Press: *The Early Works of John Dewey, 1882–1898; The Middle Works of John Dewey, 1899–1924;* and *The Later Works of John Dewey, 1925–1953.* References to these works are abbreviated as EW, MW, and LW, where, for example, EW 5: 94 indicates that the material cited or idea noted is in *The Early Works,* Volume 5, page 94.

are have formed our minds and that these configurations keep us thinking within the lines of what is, rather than releasing us to think about what could and should be (MW 13: 323). In this context, he argues that we need educational pioneers who are, at a minimum, courageous, imaginative, assertive, experimental, creative, and adventurous if we expect to extract ourselves from the pedagogical grooves that keep us traveling familiar paths. Or, we could say that Dewey asks us to fan our artistic flames so that we can sculpt other possibilities of teaching and schooling, rather than using the well-known models that are in front of us.

> ### A Reflective Opportunity
>
> If traditions and schools of thought are often inhibiting, why should we study them? Won't learning them hold back our artistic development or, at a minimum, waste our time?

But there is more to being an artist or a pioneer than may immediately be apparent. Dewey hints at part of the extra dimensions of being an artist or pioneer when he says, "They had a certain amount of dependable knowledge in mathematics and physics" (MW 13: 325). In *Art as Experience*, he claims, too, that new and aspiring artists need to understand, work within, but move beyond the great traditions or schools of thought in art; for each one offers "an organized habit of vision and of methods of ordering and conveying material" that enriches and empowers us as we grow in our own expertise (LW 10: 270). Adding these thoughts together, he seems to be saying that we as artists need a reflective understanding of our great educational traditions and a knowledge of what current disciplines have to say about teaching as well as the spirit of an artist or pedagogical pioneer.

After writing his essay "Education as Engineering," Dewey returns to the ideas of engineering and education in the treatise *The Sources of a Science of Education* (1929). This time, he refers to education as a type of social engineering (LW 5: 20). No doubt, this analogy—the teacher as social engineer—does not immediately appeal to many of us. We may not think of ourselves as engineers period, much less as social engineers. Just reading the words may cause us to wonder why Dewey would use a mechanistic illustration like social engineering to describe our work. Has he somehow forgotten that we work with human beings, not physical objects and materials? Or has he lapsed into a coercive frame of reference and decided to recommend that teachers manipulate students for a preconceived society?[1]

Let's recall that his notion of the teacher as a constructive engineer or educational pioneer does not imply that he has forgotten the human dimensions of education. Once again, it appears that he is using an analogy to suggest a key thought, not to make an exact parallel. Remembering the title of his book is a good place to begin understanding him: *The Sources of a Science of Education*. His purpose in this book is to discuss the sources, disciplines, or forms of inquiry that contribute to the development of a science of education. His use of the term *science* indicates "systematic methods of inquiry" that, "when they are brought to bear on a range of facts, enable us to understand them better and to control them more intelligently" (LW 5: 4). The general methods of inquiry, he believes, are somewhat uniform among disciplines and facilitate the development of a conceptually and empirically linked set of facts and principles that fit together and illuminate the various responsibilities of educators.

Using Dewey's definition of science, think for a moment about how you would answer the question, What are the sources of a science of education? Before you make a list, notice his use of the concept of education in this context: He includes in the notion questions that arise about curriculum, teaching, school management, and school organization and administration (LW 5: 4). Jot down your ideas regarding the disciplines that will contribute to the "systematic increase of intelligent control and understanding" (LW 5: 4) of the curriculum, teaching, management, and administration.

How many disciplines or subjects did you list? One, two, or three? Now think back to Chapter 1, in which we discussed the attempts of various people or researchers to liberate us from the dogma that teaching is an easy and simple endeavor. In that context, we mentioned research being done in the social and behavioral sciences (educational sociology, anthropology, psychology), the humanistic disciplines (educational philosophy, history, politics, ethics), the medical sciences (pediatrics, psychiatry, neurology), and the learning and teaching sciences (the methods of teaching and learning reading, mathematics, biology, history, art). This research makes it manifest that teaching is a complex and complicated undertaking. The wise mother and the wise teacher draw on a rich body of knowledge that informs their judgments and behaviors. Pulling these ideas together into a coherent whole is what many today call developing an educational theory or philosophy. Dewey uses the same terminology at times for this activity, but he also calls the synthesis a *science of education*. Thus, he titles his significant monograph on the topic *The Sources of a Science of*

Table 9.1   The Sources of an Educational Theory: A Preliminary View

Fields of Inquiry and Creativity	Examples	Illustrative Topics
Social and behavioral sciences	Educational sociology, anthropology, psychology	Understanding the cultures, languages, religions, histories, and development of students and their effects on group and individual learning in and outside of school
Humanistic disciplines	Educational philosophy, history, ethics	Understanding the social, critical, interpretative, intellectual, and evaluative issues in education and their influence on curricular, administrative, pedagogical, and personnel standards, choices, and practices
Medical sciences	Pediatrics, psychiatry, neurology	Understanding the biological, physical, and emotional development of students and their implications for educational practice
Teaching and learning sciences	Methods of teaching and learning specific skills and content	Understanding the most economical, efficient, effective, and ethical ways of teaching art, languages, literacy, math, social studies, music, science, and health education

Education. Table 9.1 captures some of his thinking about the sources of a science of education. We employ the words *educational theory* rather than *science of education* to reflect contemporary usage. In addition, Table 9.1 restates the contributing disciplines that were noted in Chapter 1.

Now let's review the disciplines that appear on Dewey's list: social psychology, biology, psychology, sociology, statistics, philosophy, psychiatry, and biological psychology (LW 5: 19–35). How does your list differ from his? Does it matter that we differ? In one sense, the differences don't matter, for Dewey thinks that the sources of a science of education include "any portions of ascertained knowledge that enter into the heart, head and hands of educators, and which, by entering in, render the performance of the educational function more enlightened, more humane, more truly educational than it was before" (LW 5: 39). In another sense, what we have on our lists is critical because we do not want to neglect important scholarly contributions that will help make us feel, think, and operate in ways that make us more perceptive, compassionate, and educative. The fact that so many fields contribute to an educational theory is important in understanding the many variables that influence and clarify the complexities of schooling, teaching, and learning (LW 5: 25). Dewey's use of the phrase "science of education," therefore, implies much more than the social and behavioral sciences. Today, the phrase is somewhat misleading. It is more appropriate to speak of educational theory or, in a few circles, a philosophy of education. Dewey, as we noted earlier, uses these two designations at times. Naturally, the phrase we use is less important than the sources of knowledge. People who do not understand the challenges of teaching and the multiple disciplines that illuminate the art of teaching are more likely to think teaching is simple and easy. They are also less capable of drawing on the appropriate knowledge as they seek to set educational policy or address school and classroom problems.

> **A Teacher Snapshot**
>
> Focus your attention on a couple of teachers who may be able to make the greatest contributions to you as a practicing or aspiring teacher. What have you already learned or what do you expect to learn from them? What distinguishes these teachers from those who have less to offer?

Discontinuing this strand of thought for a moment may prove helpful. We've been talking about the disciplines that contribute to developing an informed and reflective art of education, and, ultimately, artistic teacher. But Dewey thinks we have left out a major contributor: the ideas of reflective practitioners. Metaphorically, he suggests that the best thinking of teachers is a "neglected field" or an "almost unworked mine" (LW 5: 23), but one that must be tapped if we are to have a practical theory of education. Reinforcing the grounds for his opinion but also sounding a note of caution about the way teachers are prepared, he writes:

> Teachers are the ones in direct contact with pupils and hence the ones through whom the results of scientific findings finally reach students. They are the channels through which the consequences of educational theory come into the lives of those at school. I suspect that if these teachers are mainly channels of reception and transmission, the conclusions of science will be badly deflected and distorted before they get into the minds of pupils. (LW 5: 24)

If we agree with Dewey, we may wish to make at least two educational vows to go along with our current vows of poverty and tolerance (for those who promise to keep us poor): (1) Never underestimate or ignore the contributions of reflective teachers—including our own—as we develop our educational theory, and (2) never underestimate or ignore the contributions of unreflective preparation programs as we develop aspiring and practicing teachers. The first point is related to developing a workable or applicable educational theory. Dewey, like us, doesn't care a bit for an educational theory that is incapable of being applied to teaching and learning. But he cautions us about looking for teaching recipes and rules as a substitute for thinking. Yet there is no substitute for the minds and voices of teachers: They are always needed if what we are attempting to learn and implement is going to work effectively with children and youth in schools. Can he make it any more clear than when he asserts, "If there is any work in the world that requires the conservation of what is good in experience so that it may become an integral part of further experience, it is that of teaching" (LW 11: 224). To be consistent with the spirit of Dewey's thinking, then, we need to revise Table 9.1. Table 9.2 moves us closer to his point of view with the addition of the final category.

The second point concerns preparing and developing teachers in ways that do not use our reflective, analytical, interpretive, and synthetic abilities. When future and current teachers are viewed as "channels of reception and transmission" (LW 5: 24), we can't expect even the best scientific research and philosophical reflection to be valued by them or influence learning and schooling positively. Educators, whether university professors or district personnel, who attempt to pour ideas, data, theories, philosophies, values, plans, and strategies into teachers are not only doing an injustice to research and reflective thought but are also ensuring that what we teach will be more likely to be "badly deflected and distorted" (LW 5: 24). In the process of attempting to channel our founded beliefs and findings or theories of education, we unconsciously discredit ourselves as professionals and treat

An Introspective Moment

Can you identify any ready-made phrases, clichés, or questions that you use when criticizing or dismissing the ideas of others? Focus on one. Assume you are talking to a friend who disagrees with your cliché. How would she criticize your ready-made criticism? Does she make important points?

Table 9.2   The Sources of an Educational Theory: A Revised View

Fields of Inquiry and Creativity	Examples	Illustrative Topics
Social and behavioral sciences	Educational sociology, anthropology, psychology	Understanding the cultures, languages, religions, histories, and development of students and their effects on group and individual learning in and outside of school
Humanistic disciplines	Educational philosophy, history, ethics	Understanding the social, critical, interpretative, intellectual, and evaluative issues in education and their influence on curricular, administrative, pedagogical, and personnel standards, choices, and practices
Medical sciences	Pediatrics, psychiatry, neurology	Understanding the biological, physical, and emotional development of students and their implications for educational practice
Teaching and learning sciences	Methods of teaching and learning specific skills and content	Understanding the most economical, efficient, effective, and ethical ways of teaching art, languages, literacy, math, social studies, music, science, and health education
Reflection of practitioners	Teachers and administrators	Understanding the everyday lives of educators and students, the insights learned in the application of theory and research to practice, and the methods used by practitioners to better understand their art, students, cultures, and school ethos

teachers as mere channels—conduits or ditches of untried, unassimilated, and unappreciated information. We disrespect the very ideas and people we know are so valuable.

When we treat teachers as conduits of information, we leave the impression that universities and schools are "pipe-lines and delivery wagons" (LW 5: 131). Perhaps now is an appropriate time to refer back to a previously made comment: The minds and voices of teachers are always needed if what we are attempting to learn and implement is going to work effectively with children and youth in schools. As Dewey stresses, "A certain amount of downright thinking going on quietly in the head is as necessary to the development of any science as is the activity of the senses and the hands in the laboratory" (LW 5: 21–22). We need to do some "downright thinking" about the thinking and experience of practitioners, but as we cultivate thinking about our thinking, Dewey reminds us that criticizing our thinking is one of our major responsibilities and that we should be skeptical of any criticism that comes "ready-made" (LW 5: 134).

By now you may be wondering why we have turned from studying the art of teaching to educational theory. In response, we can paraphrase Dewey by saying that we need to select ideas and information from educational theory so that we can think more intelligently about teaching itself or the activity of teaching as an art. So teaching, like engineering, is an art that depends on other disciplines to inform it. Without an educational theory or science, a rich, reflective, and creative art of education is highly unlikely (LW 5: 6, 17, 20). Thinking—based on the contributions of an educational theory and, thereby, an art of education—is "the final source of all progress" in every aspect of education (LW 5: 40). By implication, then, teaching, like engineering, is "an art that progressively incorporates more and more of science" into the educational theory that supports and enables it (LW 5: 6). A well-developed, healthy, and growing educational theory provides invaluable insight into the art of teaching. But teaching becomes an art as the teacher passionately pursues her responsibilities with intelligence, imagination, and skill.

Throughout *The Sources of a Science of Education*, Dewey attempts to demonstrate how thinking that is based on the disciplines he mentions will enable the educator to be a more insightful curriculum builder, classroom teacher, school and classroom manager, and administrator. He especially spends time looking at the contributions of a few disciplines—particularly what he terms philosophy, psychology, psychiatry, and sociology—that he believes will help change our theory and practice as educators. Negatively, he argues:

- teaching should not be judged by immediate results, regardless of whether they are measured by "order in the class-room, correct recitations by pupils in assigned lessons, passing of examinations, [or] promotion of pupils to a higher grade" (LW 5: 7);
- the science of education cannot be viewed as "a guarantee [much like one] that goes with the sale of goods [but] rather . . . [should be seen] as a light to the eyes and a lamp to the feet" (LW 5: 7);

- the conclusions of scientific research [whether educational psychology, sociology, philosophy, or psychiatry] cannot be transformed into immediate rules of teaching and classroom management for practitioners (LW 5: 9); and
- an educational theory and an art of teaching is never completed, because the process of developing and refining them is an unending one (LW 5: 39).

Positively, he makes the case that studying the disciplines that contribute to an educational theory should result in a changed attitude and, ultimately, a system of connected ideas, facts, principles, and laws (LW 5: 10). In particular, the changed orientation means that

- the teacher will be more alert and "make certain observations which would otherwise escape" her (LW 5: 9);
- the teacher will be better able to interpret "facts which would otherwise be confused and misunderstood" (LW 5: 9);
- the teacher will have "new points of view and a wider field of observation" than she otherwise would have had (LW 5: 9);
- the teacher will filter and synthesize ideas until "they reinforce and extend one another, and in time lead to the detection of principles that bind together a number of facts" (LW 5: 10);
- the teacher will be more observant of a larger number of factors that influence her teaching and students' learning and modify and improve her work in the light of these observations (LW 5: 14–15); and
- the teacher will cultivate and rely on her ability to make informed judgments about what to do rather than simply adhering to pedagogical recipes, routines, rules, and regulations (LW 5: 15, 20–24).

QUOTES AND QUESTIONS

In *Art as Experience*, Dewey speaks of the need for the living to talk with the dead and the negative consequences of the lack of their interaction. He then makes a seemingly innocuous but, on reflection, perhaps surprising if not shocking assertion:

An individual's desires take shape under the influence of the human environment. The materials of his thought and belief come to him from others with whom he lives. He would be poorer than a beast of the fields were it not for traditions that become a part of his mind, and for institutions that penetrate below his outward actions into his purposes and satisfactions. Expression of experience is public and communicating because the experiences expressed are what they are because of experiences of the living and the dead that have shaped them. (LW 10: 274–275)

In context, he is arguing for the importance of understanding how past social history and traditions influence and inform us. This thesis is argued at the conclusion of a discussion of the human contributions to developing aesthetic experiences and artistic sensitivities. If we apply his comment to a teacher unacquainted with the intellectual and social traditions of education, is he implying that the person who is unaware of the social history of education is "poorer than a beast of the fields"? If he is, what does he mean? Is he speaking literally or hyperbolically?

A major interest for Dewey comes through clearly in his discussion of the sources of an educational theory: a philosophy of education. He says, among other things, that philosophy is a form of criticism that "differs from other criticism only in trying to carry it further and to pursue it methodically," that its disclosures are found by "pushing any investigation of familiar objects beyond the point of previous acquaintance," and that it "strives to introduce definiteness, clarity, and order" on a broad scale (LW 5: 141). Moreover, he ties creativity—an important dimension of artistic teaching—to criticism or philosophy: "Creative activity is our great need; but criticism, self-criticism, is the road to its release" (LW 5: 141). What do you think of this claim? Is self-criticism that valuable? Do you know of other scholars who tie together self-criticism and creative thinking?

IMPLICATIONS FOR THE TEACHER

As we think back through Dewey's ideas, we will take a different approach to classroom implications. As a starter, we may wish to think about our studies as a teacher. To what degree have we been introduced to and evaluated the social and intellectual traditions of our profession? In addition, to what degree have we been introduced to contemporary educational theories or humanistic and scientific research? Second, we may wish to think about the professional development workshops and graduate studies we have pursued, if we are practicing teachers. How often and to what degree is the voice of the practitioner heard and valued? Do our studies nurture a reflective science and art of teaching, or do they focus on educational recipes, routines, rules, and regulations? Is time and attention given to learning about, thinking with, and applying the theories and research we learn? Do we want to be marvelously talented pedagogical chefs, or are we satisfied being slightly dedicated educational cooks (MW 15: 186)?

Another perspective on practical implications is to ask ourselves what Dewey tells us about being an artistic teacher that is new. First, does he tell us that we'll have a better foundation for being artistic educators if we develop and keep developing an educational theory that is carefully and thoughtfully fed by—if we use contemporary terminology—selected courses and readings in educational theory, sociology of education, educational psychology, philosophy of education, abnormal psychology, curriculum theory, and personality theory? Second, does he suggest that studying these subjects alone is sufficient? Do we also need to study the sciences of teaching and learning? Moreover, do we need to think in a more comprehensive, holistic way about teaching and schooling? Third, does he imply that as we become more critical, including being critical of the familiar in our own thinking and practice, we are contributing to our potential to become more creative in our thinking and teaching? Put another way, is he saying that we are less likely to become more creative if we are not also developing our philosophical or critical abilities?

Finally, we want to ask you to do what Dewey does—or rather, doesn't do—in *The Sources of a Science of Education*. He tells us what he thinks are the main disciplines that contribute to or are the sources of a science of education. He also shares his thoughts about how a science of education—a systematic inquiry into education—contributes to and furthers the art of teaching. But he doesn't write a comparable book entitled *The Sources of an Art of Education*. Even so, we can begin writing our own work on the subject by using what we have picked up from him and adding our own thoughts. What are the immediate sources that come to mind, other than the disciplines he mentions when discussing a science of education? What other sources should be added? Do we need to know more about, say, music, art, sculpture, or drama? Will understanding the art of nature assist us as we think about the art of teaching? What can we learn that will make us better social engineers or educational theorists? Given your mental list of sources, what implications do you see for your future professional growth as a teacher?

A SUMMATIVE EXERCISE

Chapter 9   The Teacher as Social Engineer

Understandings	Qualities	Activities

READINGS

"Construction and Criticism," (LW 5: 127–143).
"Progressive Education and the Science of Education," (LW 3: 257–268).
The Sources of a Science of Education (LW 5: 1–40).

NOTE

1. Although the immediate context is concerned with the teacher understanding a science of education or educational theory and not with her becoming a social engineer who programs the lives of students, both Dewey's critics and his proponents have sometimes cautioned that his ideas regarding personhood, community, and education may undermine agency, autonomy, and individuality. Discussions of community and individuality in his writings acknowledge these interpretative problems, although he ultimately rejects the idea that either democracy or education is concerned with social or individual coercion, manipulation, or programming.

TEN

The Teacher as Composer

The real work of an artist is to build up an experience that is coherent in perception while moving with constant change in its development.

—John Dewey (LW 10: 57)

A s we noted in our discussion of the wise mother and teacher, the right understanding of experience, for Dewey, plays a critically important role in both education and art. Our ideas of experience, *an* experience, and aesthetic experiences change our perceptions, purposes, and behaviors. We see and understand differently as a result of entering these spheres. Now we can contextualize these and related ideas, elaborate on their importance to education, and discuss the role of the teacher in creating an environment that helps her compose educative experiences for all of the children in her classes.

We begin by observing that Dewey thinks that experience is ordinary and universal from one point of view. Yet his view of experience isn't what many of us think of when we hear the term. Repeatedly, therefore, he moves us

Authors' Note: References to works by John Dewey are from the collection of his works published by Southern Illinois University Press: *The Early Works of John Dewey,* 1882–1898; *The Middle Works of John Dewey,* 1899–1924; and *The Later Works of John Dewey,* 1925–1953. References to these works are abbreviated as EW, MW, and LW, where, for example, EW 5: 94 indicates that the material cited or idea noted is in *The Early Works,* Volume 5, page 94.

toward an understanding of his particular interpretation of experience. *Art as Experience* ties ordinary experience to interacting in environments:

> Experience occurs continuously, because the interaction of live creature and environing conditions is involved in the very process of living. Under conditions of resistance and conflict, aspects and elements of the self and world that are implicated in this interaction qualify experience with emotion and ideas so that conscious intent emerges. (LW 10: 42)

We can see that Dewey associates a number of specific thoughts with ordinary experience. He identifies, for example, resistance and conflict as stimulants for conscious intent. He refers to our interaction with the material and human world around us. So, too, he mentions that emotions and ideas become attached to or qualify the experiences we have. He associates experience with our interacting in our surroundings, developing intentions, and having emotions and ideas. But isn't all of this rather common knowledge? Is there a problem here that we're missing?

Strangely enough, there is a problem. As our previous glimpse indicates, Dewey fills this common term—*experience*—with ideas that make it pregnant with meaning, and this leads to problems that would not usually occur for us. In *Democracy and Education*, he directs our attention to a couple of these problems. To begin with, he contends that "the fundamental fallacy in methods of instruction lies in supposing that experience on the part of pupils may be assumed" (MW 9: 160). Assuming that students have experiences is the fundamental fallacy of teaching? Can he really mean what he says? Yes, he actually does. We shall see why he thinks this way in a moment. For now, let's look at another detail of his thinking that somewhat clarifies the value he places on the concept of experience.

The detail he adds is that the "physical equipment and arrangements of the average schoolroom are *hostile* to the existence of real situations of experience" (MW 9: 162; italics added). Schools are hostile to students having experiences? This comment seems like an exaggeration at best, but we need to move further to determine if it is. We will summarize the two matters that concern Dewey before we move to new terrain: (1) the false assumption that students are actually having experiences in class and (2) the fact that many schools are actually opposed to genuine experiences. In combination, then, he thinks our work is based on an untrue assumption and occurs in places that do not facilitate students' having experiences. Incidentally, by "arrangements,"

Dewey means everything from classroom layout to the methodological practices of the teacher, not just the way the furniture and equipment are arranged. In essence, then, Dewey says our schools are often hostile to students' having experiences, and it is a giant mistake to think students are having experiences at school. We might be thinking along the same lines if we said that the experiences students have in school often don't have much educational potential or that they are likely to teach students the wrong lessons.

If he is accurate about these two points, then, we do seem to have a problem of major proportions: We operate on a false assumption about students having experiences in classrooms. In reality, our schools are actually designed to exclude experiences. If so, it is no wonder that schooling is neither enjoyable nor effective, much less aesthetically fulfilling. But agreeing with Dewey may make us a little uneasy. Can we truthfully make these claims? What reasons and evidence do we have for them? How does Dewey defend his conclusions? Does he have any cogent evidence and arguments to support his claims?

Maybe we should start from another frame of reference with a different question: Is there more to Dewey's story than we have heard? Unquestionably, we have missed key points of Dewey's interpretation or understanding of the concept of experience. Actually, we have missed a great deal, for the story is much longer, more like a series of short stories. But we'll stick to a few rudiments. As a starter, observe that Dewey thinks experience is something we have in "the very process of living" (LW 10: 42), but that many schools don't embrace the "conditions and the situations of active contact with things and persons" like those we find in "the home, on the playground, in fulfilling of ordinary responsibilities of life" (MW 9: 162). Experience, education, and even art are or should be a customary part of life, not segregated from it in isolated places and institutions. A chapter of Dewey's story, then, is that many schools do not welcome ordinary life activities and interactions. They set up artificial or contrived arrangements that actually inhibit genuine experiences of the kind Dewey envisions. His condemnation of this segregation in art is blunt: "As long as art is the beauty parlor of civilization, neither art nor civilization is secure" (LW 10: 346). If he were talking about education, he might exclaim, "As long as education is isolated in the school, neither education nor civilization is safe!" Artificial experiences anywhere are at best noneducative and at worst miseducative.

Another chapter in Dewey's story is seen as we look at the following list of experientially related terms, some of which we saw earlier. Keep in mind,

Figure 10.1   Continuum of Pseudo- and Authentic Experiences

however, that the word *experience* is used only in a courtesy sense in the first two instances, for there aren't interactions of the kind Dewey thinks are essential to genuine experience. The five terms or phrases are (1) *anesthetic experience*, (2) *non-aesthetic experience*, (3) *experience*, (4) *an experience*, and (5) *aesthetic experience*. A helpful or useful way of understanding these five conceptions is thinking of them as extending along a progressively positive continuum from left to right, as Figure 10.1 suggests.

This continuum, however, may be somewhat misleading, for anesthetic and non-aesthetic experiences are, perhaps, on a scale of their own. In reality, they may belong on a nonexperiential continuum. That is to say, there is little to nothing about them that can be meaningfully termed *experience*. They are, in reality, pseudo-experiences. With this background, we can now fill in some of the gaps in Dewey's story about experience and our responsibilities as teachers. We will examine the five concepts as we continue his story.

First, it is apparent that we don't need much explanation of an *anesthetic experience* (LW 10: 47). We've had them; we've contributed to them; we've caused them; we've interrupted them; we've even enjoyed them, dozing in the sun occasionally. Indeed, we may have actually had an anesthetic experience in the last paragraph or two! Still, we may have questions about whether the inactivity or sleep induced—or we might say, the intellectual resting and gliding that is occurring—is caused by us, students, schools, districts, others, or a combination of factors. But if we are characterized by a "passionate excitement" about our teaching fields and a love of being with our students, it is difficult to believe that we'll remain very long at this point on the continuum (LW 10: 70). Whether the cause or causes of pedagogy-induced sleep are the anesthetic we provide in our classes or a systemic disease in our school, we need to focus on the challenges of teaching and get back to being artists in the classroom. Dozing or contributing to an anesthetic experience may sometimes be unavoidable. Running an academic motel is avoidable. If we don't enjoy brain waves and moving bodies, we should re-create ourselves as forensic scientists or morticians.

Second, *non-aesthetic experience* may be distinguished by the activities that occur at one or both of two poles: "At one pole is the loose succession [of activity] that does not begin at any particular place and that ends . . . at no particular place" and at the other pole we find inactivity, "arrest, constriction, proceeding from parts having only a mechanical connection with one another" (LW 10: 47). The first pole may be characterized by activity and even change, but these events are not connected to intentions and ends, and they don't move students toward a unitary or coherent understanding of what they have learned. Students may be busy, but they are simply engaged in cognitive doodling and roving. They learn a little, make a few connections to their lives, and find no meaningful application to their worlds. The second pole also lacks connection to everyday life and, consequently, leads to a deterioration of both interest and meaning in activities. In time, activity itself is restricted, if not terminated, by students. They drop out physically or mentally. Fully developed, the second pole appears to be virtually synonymous with anesthetic experience.

Dewey's third idea is *experience*, and he indirectly clarifies it in the previous quote with allusions to beginnings and endings, and parts and connections. But Dewey thinks that experience may be on a lower level than this—beneath a clear understanding and connection of beginnings and endings—not necessarily conscious, but not as far down as some places on the anesthetic and non-aesthetic levels. Similar to the first pole of the non-aesthetic level, students are active, but they also have intentional beginnings, go in the direction of identified ends, and make some connections along the way. They can feel something developing even if they can't say what.

> ### A Teacher Snapshot
>
> Do you recall a teacher who "just seemed to know" when you mentally escaped from her class and were in another part of your environment? What was she like? Did she know students better than other teachers? If yes, do you know why she knew you better?

But they are distracted from their goals and, as a result, they waste their energy and much of the limited insight they gain. This waste occurs when

what we observe and what we think, what we desire and what we get, are at odds with each other. We put our hands to the plow and turn back; we start and then we stop, not because the experience has reached the end for the sake of which it was initiated but because of extraneous interruptions or of inner lethargy. (LW 10: 42)

So, students may go through the entire day learning bits and pieces of information and, at times, sensing a couple of connections or their beginnings, but they may have no particular goals or ends toward which they are moving. They are basically school attendees, not students in any serious sense of the word. For instance, students may merely go to school, pursue whatever ideas or activities interest them at the moment, enjoy social lives with their classmates, think about an upcoming date or athletic event, ignore the people who irritate or offend them, and think ahead of responsibilities as athletes, cheerleaders, club members, or employees. Maybe they think about an abusive caregiver, a medical need, or an unwanted pregnancy. After school, they may go to cheerleading practice or the grocery store before returning home to do the laundry, watch a television program, surf the Internet, or vacuum a couple of rooms. The next day is more of the same. Of course, there are much worse scenarios that we could sketch.

Imagining this scenario helps us understand what Dewey means when he writes, "What we observe and . . . think, what we desire and . . . get, are at odds" (LW 10: 42). As teachers, we stop and start; we are interrupted, then return to cold questions; ideas emerge and disappear; comments are made but have to be ignored; connections are rare, superficial, or partial; closure is uncommon. The day ends with a flutter of emotions and scampering thoughts. Having these kinds of experiences, then, falls far below our ideals. If students only have these kinds of experiences, schools struggle to give them powerful and meaningful experiences. If schools—never mind homes and communities—are arranged in ways that throw additional obstacles into the mix, the challenges for the teacher mount and, in many cases, even the already inadequate learning of students is diminished. The challenges may simply be insurmountable, at least for most people most of the time.

Of course, there are authentic experiences—or, better, for Dewey, just experiences—and they provide meaningful learning and educative opportunities. Students and teachers interpret, synthesize, discover, integrate, apply, construct, and rethink what they are learning. Conceptual connections are made in and among classes and courses and with external personal, social, political, religious, and economic events. When speaking of experience in this sense, he argues that it must meet at least two criteria: (1) the principle of continuity and (2) the principle of interaction. If the principle of continuity of experience is met, it means that "every experience both takes up something from those which have gone before and modifies in some way the quality of those which come after" (LW 13: 19). But this principle is meaningless by itself, for every situation contains a degree of continuity between the past, present, and future. The principle of continuity becomes valuable when it is informed by Dewey's notion of growth. Does the experience retard or promote growth in specific and general situations? Does it enable personal and community growth? Learning that is based on the relevant past, that can be applied to present problems, and that helps us understand and control the future meets the criterion of continuity.

The principle of interaction informs both continuity and growth. Dewey thinks of the interaction of the student with her environment when he explains this concept. Instead of emphasizing the objective or external world and the forms of inquiry and people that assist us in understanding it, or emphasizing the subjective or internal world of the student and her inclinations and emotions, Dewey maintains that experience involves both: Interaction between the student and the environment is demanded, and exploration and reflection on one's inner inclinations, feelings, beliefs, and thoughts are similarly required. Neither dimension should be slighted by educators. The teacher has the responsibility of both selecting from the objective world that which is suitable for a student and understanding a student's readiness for particular experiences. Similarly, the teacher is responsible for nurturing a twofold adaptation:

> The principle of interaction makes it clear that failure of adaptation of material to needs and capacities of individuals may cause an experience to be non-educative quite as much as failure of an individual to adapt himself to the material. (LW 13: 27)

These ideas about continuity and interaction—which often include artistic and aesthetic elements—bring us closer to what Dewey refers to as *an* experience.

Dewey's concept of experience, therefore, seems progressively more desirable after we pass through anesthetic experience and non-aesthetic experience and approach *an* experience and aesthetic experience. The trip to *an* experience and aesthetic experience is both challenging and stimulating, and the rich rewards are worth the time and effort. But we must pause to ask, what do *an* experience and aesthetic experience offer us that makes the journey—sometimes a very tiring, if periodically and ultimately enjoyable, trip—worthwhile? The answer to this question is discovered as we revisit and learn more about what Dewey means by *an* experience and aesthetic experience.

You can tell by the way we—following Dewey—italicize *an* that *an* experience is noteworthy. The statement "That's an experience I'll never forget" illuminates his meaning. When we make this statement in a positive way, we are usually implying several things: The experience was memorable, satisfying, and enjoyable. It opened our eyes and reshaped the way we understand. Nothing else is needed to make the experience complete, although we can always learn more from later ones. This learning experience is *an* experience, one that offers us much and is recommended to others. Other ideas clarify what *an* experience is to Dewey: It is integrated, fulfilling, rounded out, whole, self-sufficient, and consummated. The parts are brought together into a meaningful and rewarding whole that allows new ways of perceiving. Closure and fulfillment characterize the outcome (LW 10: 42). Students and teachers who have this kind of experience are excited about the potential of having similar ones in the future.

Finally, we look at *aesthetic experience*. Aesthetic experience is experience, the type of experience that both the artist or teacher and the audience or student have when both are prepared for a great performance. It is the kind of experience that a teacher and students have when they are prepared for and enter into a stunning learning encounter. But what is the experience itself? How may we describe it? We begin by going back to the idea of *an* experience, because an aesthetic experience grows out of, extends, and enlarges it: It is memorable, satisfying, enjoyable, and complete. It is also integrated, fulfilling, finished, rounded, whole, self-sufficient, and consummated. Dewey tells us that aesthetic experience extends farther, however, and involves getting the most out of "the process of production" (LW 11: 539)—whether it is participating in a symphonic production, engaging in a classroom discussion, or constructing a home for a charitable organization. More specifically, an aesthetic experience includes a "degree of completeness of living in the experience of making and of perceiving that makes the difference between what is . . . esthetic . . . and what is not" (LW 10: 33). Notice the phrase "the experience of making and perceiving." An aesthetic experience involves making or doing something and seeing or understanding differently as a consequence of the activity. The extent to which both the teacher and the student enter into both the artistic process and the aesthetic outcome determines their degree of satisfaction, integration, and consummation. Neither the artist nor the teacher can do it alone. So the artistic and the aesthetic are linked, but aesthetic perception or new understanding, enjoyment, and appreciation are the outcomes, foremost for the student but also for the teacher. Importantly, the factors involved in an aesthetic experience are more clear and intense than in *an* experience and are "lifted above the threshold of perception and are made manifest for their own sake" (LW 10: 53, 62–63).

To come to the point, an aesthetic experience is a holistic one that takes us to a deeper understanding and more enjoyable appreciation of what we learn, regardless of whether it is historical, scientific, literary, musical, artistic, or mathematical. At this time, we may feel that we have never had an aesthetic experience and know that our students haven't! But we have all had and continue to have aesthetic experiences, although we may not have labeled them such. Our cultures, Dewey says, make us think that aesthetic experiences are part of high culture: that they only occur in museums, galleries, cathedrals, and symphony halls. We assume that they don't take place in everyday affairs while we are playing, talking, walking, watching, sitting, reading, or thinking much less in the barren prisons that society calls schools. But there is no reason to think this, Dewey says, and our cultures have been misleading us.

Ordinary experience—a hike up to a mountain vista, a walk through the park, an afternoon studying paintings, a weekend retreat to meditate, a tuning of an engine, an evening at a concert, a conversation with a friend, a final coat of paint on the house, an hour with a poem, a walk through fall foliage, a sitting down at the dinner table with family, a trip down a snowy slope, or an encounter with a short story—may and often does involve aesthetic elements. When they constitute an aesthetic experience, they are fulfilling and valued in their own right. But they can also be educational. In fact, it is hard to see how they couldn't also be. The intense and rich messages and perceptions gained from these experiences explain why Dewey thinks "art becomes the incomparable organ of instruction" (LW 10: 349). No doubt we should clarify that he appears to speak of the art we usually find in museums. But how could he or we exclude art as a pedagogical activity or as an educational work? When teaching is artistic and learning is aesthetic, the educative experience is "incomparable" (LW 10: 349). The solution, of course, is not to move schools into museums and galleries, but to make our teaching and students' learning more like art, more of an artistic, aesthetic experience. The more we compose such experiences, the more influential teaching and learning are. But we must recognize that art cannot be confined to the classroom, gallery, or mountaintop if students and adults are to enjoy aesthetically rewarding lives. Art must enter into the lives of ordinary people and saturate "their homes; their furnishings and utensils; their walls, hangings, floor coverings, tables and chairs; the dishes from which they eat and those with which they cook" (LW 11: 521–522). As society and culture become aware of and experience the aesthetic in everyday life, the potential of artistic teaching is more fully realized.

Strangely, maybe, we frequently have difficulty explaining to ourselves as well as to others exactly what it was that excited us so much, flooded us with new insights, shaped our feelings, or altered our relationships with others when we have an aesthetic experience. The difficulty we have in explaining these experiences is influenced by several factors. For example, we've never thought of them as aesthetic in many cases, so we don't search for such terms to shed light on our lives and our teaching. In addition, the problem results, in part, because we look for elements in the experience that will explain it. But the parts of an aesthetic experience or *an* experience don't capture the whole or completeness that makes an experience. When we talk about a few pieces of our experiences, we cannot easily add them up to convey the whole experience. Plus, the consummating flow, movement, or moment of an aesthetic experience is usually too complex to describe in a few sentences, especially when our aesthetic vocabulary is undeveloped, as it often is in cultures that see art of any kind as a frill or extra, a prerogative of a rich, leisured class.

An additional reason it is difficult to explain the aesthetic is that such experiences cannot be adequately captured with prose. Sculptures, dances, photographs, and poems cannot be reduced to prose. The feelings and emotions they stir cannot be adequately or completely captured with words. As a result, there is a sense in which not only a picture but a dramatic production or short poem is worth a thousand words. We may say or hear, accordingly, statements such as: "I don't know how to explain it. You'll have to do it yourself." Or we may just say, "It was an experience that I cannot explain. You'll have to take the course yourself." A few of Dewey's attempts

---

A Reflective Opportunity

On a scale of 1 to 10 (with 10 being the least desirable), how would you rate the anti-experience influence of the classrooms you experienced when you were in preschool through 12th grade? Was there a great deal of variability?

---

to describe such experiences include, among others, such phrases as "being fully alive," "complete interpenetration of self and the world," "heightened vitality," and "expanding and enriched life" (LW 10: 25, 34).

A trip back to Dewey's two earlier claims now seems appropriate. Consider what he said: We make a huge error when we (1) assume that students are actually having experiences (of the *an* experience and aesthetic experience variety) in class and when we (2) create classrooms that are conducted so that they are anything but real. His claims now appear reasonable, but what they report is unfortunate.

QUOTES AND QUESTIONS

Dewey makes an interesting comment about what he thinks most of us lack to become well-developed artists, and the comment may apply to pedagogical as well as to other artists:

> What most of us lack in order to be artists is not the inceptive emotion, nor yet merely technical skill in execution. It is capacity to work a vague idea and emotion over into terms of some definite medium. Were expression but a kind of decalcomania, or a conjuring of a rabbit out of the place where it lies hid, artistic expression would be a comparatively simple matter. But between conception and bringing to birth there lies a long period of gestation. During this period inner material of emotion and idea is as much transformed through acting and being acted upon by objective material as the latter undergoes modification when it becomes a medium of expression. (LW 10: 82)

No wonder we sometimes talk of born or gifted teachers and think of some methods courses as unhelpful. Notice the progression suggested by Dewey's words. First, note the ideas associated with having a baby: conception, gestation, and delivery. Second, note the words that suggest a gradual change: transformation and modification.

Third, observe that there is an interaction that occurs: acting and being acted on. Fourth, look at the words that imply what is being changed and delivered: a vague idea and emotion or the inner material of emotion and idea. Think silently for a second. Is Dewey right? What do you consider your greatest challenges when it comes to being an educational artist? Are your challenges similar to those of other teachers? How do your and their challenges compare with the ones identified by Dewey?

Let's think from a negative point of view for a moment. Dewey nominates a number of behaviors for the Enemies of Aesthetic Experience Award. He believes that they are detrimental to the development of aesthetic experience, regardless of whether we are involved in educational or formal learning activities. His precise comment may be useful in helping us plan to avoid anesthetic and non-aesthetic experiences:

> The enemies of the esthetic are neither the practical nor the intellectual. They are the humdrum; slackness of loose ends; submission to convention in practice and intellectual procedure. Rigid abstinence, coerced submission, tightness on one side and dissipation, incoherence and aimless indulgence on the other, are deviations in opposite directions from the unity of experience. (LW 10: 47)

If you were writing a parallel but positive statement about the friends of aesthetic experience, what would you say? What are the first four or five ideas that come to mind?

IMPLICATIONS FOR THE TEACHER

Some of the implications of Dewey's five views of experience are straightforward. Several emerge immediately. First of all, teaching, at one time or another, seems to include all five kinds of experiences for most if not all of us. We don't like making this confession, but neither life nor teaching is always a completely fulfilling or aesthetic experience. Yet we realize that the more we progress toward and live and teach in the spheres of *an* experience and aesthetic experience, the more educative teaching and learning are for our students and for us. A second point that we ought to keep in mind is that teaching and learning, like other arts, grow into *an* experience and into an aesthetic experience. Teaching is not, even during many very good teaching moments, sessions, and periods, always fully *an* experience, much less an aesthetic experience. Our teaching slips back and forth across the borders of experience and *an* experience. Art, learning, living, and teaching don't work in predictable and perfect

---

An Introspective Moment

Think of your most enjoyable learning experience, your most enjoyable series of learning experiences. How would you describe them? Where were you when they occurred? Were they aesthetic experiences?

ways. When we feel like we're rehearsing for a performance or teaching specific information and skills, we are probably contributing to the development of later aesthetic experiences, perhaps an educational drama, painting, song, or dance. Aesthetic experiences are built up over time as we have valuable teaching and learning opportunities. Third, some teaching and learning experiences are sprinkled with various moments of great insight, enjoyment, and growth that possess aesthetic dimensions. Experiential wholeness occurs more than once in the same engagement or discussion or activity, and a growing satisfaction, perception, and unity are noticed along the way. Aesthetic experiences almost have a life of their own, are unpredictable, and cannot be stereotyped. They appear unexpectedly and visit again without notice. They are characterized by novelty, suspense, and surprise even when anticipated.

Two other thoughts merit attention. The fourth idea comes from the previous three and from prior discussions: Time is needed to compose or build *an* experience and aesthetic experiences out of experiences. Our opening quote for this chapter suggests this notion: "The real work of an artist is to build up an experience that is coherent in perception while moving with constant change in its development" (LW 10: 57). In one sense, we don't aim at an aesthetic experience. Instead, we seek to get students engaged in educative activities that build up to *an* experience and, climactically if we are fortunate, to an aesthetic experience. The flow from a student's engagement in (a) a learning activity to (b) an educative experience to (c) *an* experience to (d) an aesthetic experience needs time to occur and mature. Many such activities are usually needed for the flow to be a regular stream and not just a trickle. Bear in mind, too, that between "conception and bringing to birth there lies a long period of gestation" (LW 10: 82).

Although Dewey aims this previous comment at the artist or teacher, it seems suitable for the audience or student, also. Gestation periods for the student are as important as those for the teacher. Maybe more important, because the student has to be prepared for what she will experience. So reflecting, thinking, observing, reading, examining, discussing, and planning are necessary if we are going to be able to ensure that students' activities are "composed into *an* experience" (LW 10: 42). Except for the artistic geniuses among us, composing classroom activities into powerful, holistic, and rich experiences takes considerable time, effort, planning, and learning. Well, this last comment is incorrect according to Dewey. He doesn't even make an allowance for the genius: "An instantaneous experience is an impossibility, biologically and psychologically. An experience is a product, one might almost say a by-product, of continuous and cumulative interaction of an organic self with the world" (LW 10: 224).

As we consider a fifth implication of Dewey's view of experience for the teacher, let's look at an observation he makes about the difference between the qualities of fine art and the signs and symbols of arts that are largely intellectual. In *Art and Experience*, he notes:

> The difference is enormous. It is one of the reasons why the strictly intellectual art will never be popular as music is popular. Nevertheless, the experience itself has a satisfying emotional quality because it possesses internal integration and fulfillment reached through ordered and organized movement. This artistic structure may be immediately felt. In so far, it is esthetic. What is even more important is that not only is this quality a significant motive in undertaking intellectual inquiry and in keeping it honest, but that no intellectual activity is an integral event (is *an* experience), unless it is rounded out with this quality. Without it, thinking is inconclusive. In short, esthetic cannot be sharply marked off from intellectual experience since the latter must bear an esthetic stamp to be itself complete. (LW 10: 45)

This comment should help us be realistic about pedagogical artistry. As an intellectual art, teaching will never be as popular as music, perhaps the most popular of arts. Nevertheless, it can be appreciated by others and satisfying to its practitioners. When it is characterized by an integrated, orderly, and fulfilling growth toward a desired goal, it bears "an esthetic stamp" and is both complete and enjoyable (LW 10: 45).

Before we rush away, look back at the quotation from *Art as Experience*. What do you see that we have ignored? Maybe we see different thoughts, but the words that surface for us are "a significant motive in undertaking intellectual inquiry and in keeping it honest" (LW 10: 45). Dewey tells us that there is a "satisfying emotional quality" that our students and we have when we are able to integrate and order our thoughts. The satisfaction of integrated thinking is also a motivating force to learn more and to keep our thinking honest. Perhaps it is also a motive—or, better, motivating force—as we plan activities, engagements, and experiences and seek to compose them into *an* experience or, even, an aesthetic experience.

A SUMMATIVE EXERCISE

Chapter 10   The Teacher as Composer

Understandings	*Qualities*	*Activities*

READINGS

"The Act of Expression," in *Art as Experience* (LW 10: 64–87).
"Experience and Thinking," in *Democracy and Education* (MW 9: 146–158).
"Having an Experience," in *Art as Experience* (LW 10: 42–63).
"Thinking in Education," in *Democracy and Education* (MW 9: 159–170).

ELEVEN

The Teacher as Wise Physician

The teacher must be a wise physician of the soul to secure proper results.

—John Dewey (EW 1: 88)

The challenges of facilitating, designing, and composing activities that progressively move a student toward having a series of experiences, *an experience,* and aesthetic experiences may seem overwhelming. We may be staggered by our responsibilities, partly because of the standards we set for ourselves, partly because we do not control students' learning and behavior, and partly because we feel pulled and pushed in so many directions by parents, principals, and others. We know, as Dewey so poignantly reminds us, that we often have less real freedom in classrooms than students do.

Authors' Note: References to works by John Dewey are from the collection of his works published by Southern Illinois University Press: *The Early Works of John Dewey, 1882–1898; The Middle Works of John Dewey, 1899–1924;* and *The Later Works of John Dewey, 1925–1953.* References to these works are abbreviated as EW, MW, and LW, where, for example, EW 5: 94 indicates that the material cited or idea noted is in *The Early Works,* Volume 5, page 94.

Our respect for them and our view of teaching and learning provides them with much freedom, but they also have the option of doing whatever they please—unless we intervene in their lives and involve them in educative activities. On the other hand, we recognize—and would even if we were not professionals—that the school, district, parents, and guardians significantly influence what we can and cannot do. The pressure, if it is not overwhelming, can be a stimulus to think and innovate and can actually provide an additional impetus to do a great job in the classroom.

We don't have to think much to realize that we too infrequently get the opportunity to practice what we know and understand in the classroom because the whole atmosphere and environment of education with its pre-scriptions, inspections, examinations, and standardizations are "the great forces working against . . . the principle of individuality in education" (MW 15: 181). Instead of letting us think and teach creatively in the light of our edu-cational theory or philosophy, the educational milieu coerces and dictates so many of our actions and, thereby, injects "a factitious factor" (MW 15:181) that gets between our students and us. So if we have the time, energy, and courage, we may try to get our school administrators and policymakers to understand the damage being done to teaching and learning and to re-envision and reorganize schools so that they actually "emancipate, assist and safeguard the individual teacher in the classroom" (MW 15: 180–181). While we are pushing this and complementary concerns, Dewey suggests that we keep creating space for ourselves in our schools and classrooms and keep our sights on the children and youth we teach. Specifically, he says that we need to become wise physicians of the souls of students.

We explored wisdom earlier when we looked at the teacher as a wise mother. So we'll sidestep the adjective and focus on the phrase "physician of the soul." But, of course, in practice it would be deadly to ignore the development and use of wisdom.

We rightly ask, "What is a physician of the soul?" because we don't use this terminology. The word *soul* implies something spiritual for many people, as it did to Dewey at the time he wrote these words. For nearly all of us, the term suggests an inner, holistic, or more complete picture of a person. If we put the idea into our language, we would say the teacher should be an astute student of the thinking, feeling, and valuing of her pupils. She needs to get beyond surface impressions to understand how a student thinks, solves problems, and feels about things. Dewey himself says that "the teacher must

Table 11.1 Early Human Impulses and Indicators

General Impulse	Sample Indicators
Social	Talking, interacting, joining
Constructive	Making, playing, forming
Investigative	Asking, exploring, inquiring
Expressive	Imagining, creating, innovating

come into the most intimate relations with the minds of the students"
(EW 1: 88). How do we, then, come to an intimate or close understanding
of the thoughts, emotions, and values of each student? A number of suggestions—or interpretative schemes—that help us see better into the mind of
each student come from Dewey. For instance, Table 5.1, Figure 6.1, and
Figure 10.1 offer methods of glimpsing into student's minds. In this chapter
and later ones, we will examine several other lenses into the minds of
students.

First, we will consider the student's native and shaped impulses. In
capsule form, this particular interpretative scheme aids in seeing each
student's common and unique impulses. In *The School and Society*, we find
Dewey's earliest and, perhaps, clearest statement about the child's impulses.
He identifies four instincts, impulses, or interests that the teacher ought
to understand, think about, and plan for as she seeks to understand children
and their learning interests. The potential for the artistic and aesthetic is
intrinsic to these impulses and may be wisely used by us as we take students
from anesthetic and non-aesthetic experiences into more desirable forms
of experience. We should stress, too, that they indicate that the nature of
the student is to be artistic; for example, impulses, especially the constructive
and expressive or artistic ones, can lead to the expression and development
of creative and innovative activities and products.

As we examine these impulses and their indicators, it is worth keeping
in mind that Dewey thinks the investigative and the expressive or artistic
impulses grow out of what he labels social and constructive impulses.
Consequently, we list them in the order in which he thinks they emerge in
Table 11.1.

Dewey believes these impulses become apparent in all children and
thinks that they are influenced by formal and informal education. Each child,

> **A Reflective Opportunity**
>
> Do you think you have identified
> some general impulses in people
> or students that Dewey doesn't
> mention? If your answer is yes,
> what actions or dispositions are
> indicators of these impulses?

therefore, should be understood in
light of the strength of each impulse
and its associated abilities. Understanding the mind of a student, therefore, includes knowing her native
impulses and developed abilities and
how they have been shaped by culture.
Is she instinctively oriented more
toward social or constructive impulses
or a combination? How do her inquiry
and expressive impulses show themselves? What do they tell us about helping
her enter into educative experiences that are holistic and aesthetic?

To understand the impulses and the mind of a person, nevertheless, means
understanding not just her impulses but her culture and education, including
prior schooling if any. How has the student's culture entered into her mind and
shaped her impulses? How has the student's previous formal education influenced her development? Where and how do we enter the picture and assist the
child or youth as she develops her abilities? The complexities of the student's
culture, education, and impulses, therefore, help create a unique mind that we
need to understand as we guide each student (MW 1: 21–32). A pause to mention a student's culture is worth the time because it is crucial that we understand it. The family, community, music, language, norms, and religion—to
mention but a few items—that help shape a student's mind are tremendously
important. Yet they present an enormous challenge to us, for we cannot be
expected to understand so much about so many students. Or can we? Whatever
our answer to this question, several things seem apparent. First, we cannot
know our future preschool through 12th-grade students when we graduate
from university, except for general ideas that we learn in both arts and sciences
and certain specialized teacher preparation courses and experiences. Second,
reflective school administrators arrange professional development activities
that center on understanding the neighborhoods, communities, children, and
youth that we serve. Understanding our teaching fields, learning theory,
human development, professional ethics, instructional technology, pedagogical techniques, societal development, and educational theory is an important
consideration for a teacher, but it really is not enough. Only professional
development after graduation can provide a serious, nonsuperficial understanding of our students' minds as they have been influenced by their native

abilities, tendencies, and cultures. To underestimate the importance of this idea is a terrible mistake, for it is to fail to realize that "the educational center of gravity is the cultural or humane aspects of the subject. From this center, any material becomes relevant in so far as it is needed to help appreciate the significance of human activities and relations" (MW 9: 220).

Dewey's notion of soul or mind is not narrowly intellectual but includes a student's feelings and purposes. The mind is not a static entity either but "a process" and "a growing affair," characterized by "distinctive phases of capacity and interest" (MW 1: 71). As a result, we cannot assume that the student we knew last year is the same one we will teach this year, much less five years later when she is a teenager. Children, like other people, change, and not just physically. But we can assume that because we teach dynamic and growing students, we do not need to draw out their ideas or pour ideas into them. Every student or child is

> already running over, spilling over, with activities of all kinds. He is not a purely latent being whom the adult had to approach with a great deal of caution and skill in order to draw out some hidden germ of activity. The child is already intensely active and the question of education is the question of taking hold of his activities, of giving them direction. Through direction, through organized use, they tend toward valuable results, instead of scattering or being left to merely impulsive expression. (MW 1: 25)

In time, Dewey modifies his interpretative scheme to include other impulses that teachers ought to take into consideration. Every impulse, however, is an opportunity for growth and educational guidance. If we design experiences in view of these tendencies and allow children to become physically active as they learn, Dewey exclaims, "Going to school is a joy, management is less of a burden, and learning is easier" (MW 9: 202). His promise to us in this realm is significant. Is it worth the extra time and effort to test his idea?

In *Experience and Education*, Dewey takes us deeper into the world of the student as he discusses the necessity of a child's impulses being converted into desires and then the desires being transformed into purposes. The processes of conversion and transformation are critical in the maturation of each student and for the teacher as she seeks to understand each one's mind (LW 13: 43–45). Determining—or at least thinking about—whether a student is moved by blind impulses (urges), developing desires (ideas), reflective purposes (plans that take

into consideration potential consequences), or some combination of these motivating forces is an invaluable step in "reading a student's mind." Overall, then,
we can say that Dewey thinks that an impulse is more like a blind urge, whereas
a purpose is a more or less thought-out plan of action. Between the two, it helps
to have a fairly clear idea of what we want to achieve, a consciously considered
desire. The processes involved in the conversion of impulses and transformation of desires are partly illustrated in Figure 11.1.

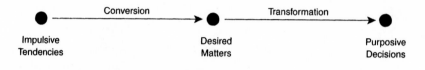

Figure 11.1   Impulse Conversion and Desire Transformation Processes

The process of moving from impulses to desires to purposes doesn't
happen automatically or simply by being born into the world and living in a
family: "The notion of a spontaneous normal development of these activities
is pure mythology. The natural, or native, powers furnish the initiating and lim-
iting forces in all education; they do not furnish its ends or aims" (MW 9: 121).
This being the case, then, the process involves a "complex intellectual operation" (LW 13: 44) that may be poorly understood by parents and other caregivers. Transformation and conversion involve

> (1) observation of surrounding conditions; (2) knowledge of what has hap-
> pened in similar situations in the past, a knowledge obtained partly by recol-
> lection and partly from the information, advice, and warning of those who
> have had a wider experience; and (3) judgment which puts together what is
> observed and what is recalled to see what they signify. A purpose differs from
> an original impulse and desire through its translation into a plan and method
> of action based upon foresight of the consequences of acting under given
> observed conditions in a certain way. (LW 13: 44)

The first point—the activity of observation—is a vital part of growth
for the student, offers insight for the teacher, and calls for understanding
the conditions and obstacles that block impulses and, eventually, provide the
opportunity for them to be converted into desires. Seeing or observing the
obstacles and the consequences of one's impulses not only lays the foundation

for impulses being converted into desires but for desires being transformed into purposes. Ideally, the student's purposes are increasingly, although not invariably, reflective, and they allow her to see the significance of several matters: (a) the meaning of what she sees, hears, touches, smells, and tastes; (b) the relevance of prior experiences and knowledge in informing a decision about the current situation; (c) the projection of probable consequences of existing options of action; and (d) the formation of a judgment about the most reasonable course of action to take. In the most basic terms, then, this means that the teacher observes the student so she can better understand her and then helps the student better understand herself.

> ## A Teacher Snapshot
>
> Do you know a teacher who is particularly effective in getting students to cooperate with her in educative activities? Is she naturally gifted, well trained, or both? Does her school need to make better use of her expertise in this area?

The teacher and the student, of course, have to collaborate or cooperate in the conversion and the transformation of impulses into desires and into purposes. But cooperation will be less than fully informed if both don't understand the conversion process and the role of obstacles as they block or inhibit impulses. On the surface, obstacles and barriers appear counterproductive, but Dewey thinks that they are essential and invaluable parts of the personal, educational, and social maturation process. To try to remove the regular or everyday obstacles from the paths of students will result in children and youth being subject to impulses and desires, not their becoming strong, independent, purposeful people. Impulses and desires are progressively joined by purposes, but purposes and linked plans are often personally oriented and do not take into consideration the needs of others and society. Conversely, the expected or desirable scenario is depicted in Figure 11.2.

| Impulses Expressed | Obstacles Occur | Desires Develop | Obstacles Occur | Purposes Selected | Obstacles Occur | Plans Pursued |

Figure 11.2   The Role of Obstacles in Personal Learning and Growth

This scenario, even when largely successful, is much like a cycle, not a simple linear progression. There are times too when a person or student does not avoid or overcome obstacles. Sometimes we are disappointed when unwanted consequences arise, but, we hope, the student is not defeated. If an intelligent and caring teacher guides her, she will have the support that she needs to return to an analysis of learning activities and plan for future actions.

QUOTES AND QUESTIONS

Dewey's analysis of conversion and transformation processes shows that it is a complex and challenging endeavor. Specifically, he says: "The crucial educational problem is that of procuring the postponement of immediate action upon desire until observation and judgment have intervened" (LW 13: 44–45). As teachers, we might disagree with Dewey's thought. Are there prior needs that are just as challenging? Or do think his interpretative scheme regarding the conversion of impulses and the transformation of desires is inaccurate?

If we agree with his basic thought, how might we help students recognize the value of postponing or delaying action? Dewey says we need the virtues of courage and persistence if we are going to be successful as teachers:

> A reorganization of education so that learning takes place in connection with the intelligent carrying forward of purposeful activities is slow work. It can only be done piecemeal, a step at a time. But this is not a reason for nominally accepting one educational philosophy and accommodating ourselves in practice to another. It is a challenge to undertake the task of reorganization courageously and to keep at it persistently. (MW 9: 144)

We know that reorganizing is a slow process. But have we ever heard that reform can only be done "piecemeal, a step at a time"? What should we make of Dewey's idea of piecemeal change? Is it any different from patching up the status quo here and there? If this is the appropriate way to think about changing a school, why do so many people talk and write about systemic and radical change? Is piecemeal change inconsistent with systemic and radical reform? Can changing pieces of the puzzle lead to a new mosaic or revolution in schooling? Can we be sure they will? Is there any other way to avoid the catastrophic consequences that sometimes follow ill-informed, badly thought out, and poorly planned reform programs?

IMPLICATIONS FOR THE TEACHER

Working with stone, paint, notes, wood, iron, glass, words, and most other art materials is in a critically important way relatively easy compared with working with humans. Direct a play. Organize a trip. Coach a basketball team. Sign with a musical group. Produce a yearbook. The human element makes art challenging, much more difficult.

> **An Introspective Moment**
>
> Do you think you are strong in the area of making judgments? Can you think of a couple of examples to support your thinking?

Working with children and youth and their caregivers is even more demanding. Making judgments about when a student is impulsive, desirous, or purposive is one thing. It is another thing to share this information with a child. To say that it is another thing to discuss it with an adolescent is a gross understatement. We are in an entirely different universe when we broach the idea with caregivers. Maybe we'd better keep our ideas to ourselves sometimes—or just share them with colleagues to get their feedback. Is this one of the places that wisdom is essential? But maybe we are such sophisticated artists at times that we will be able to weave important ideas, questions, and suggestions into conversations with students and parents. Whatever route we take will demand our greatest insight, imagination, sensitivity, creativity, grace, poise, and respect for others. Not to mention wisdom, again! We will need to see into the minds of those we're working with so that we contribute to their development and growth, not add to their frustration. Indeed, we'll need to be wise physicians of the soul, because we are looking for "proper results" (EW 1: 88), not just outcomes.

In closing, it is critical to observe that a nearly hidden but crucial implication of being a wise physician is that the teacher applies, adapts, or develops methods of getting on the inside of students, including their thinking, feeling, valuing, and choosing. In other words, we need an interpretative scheme or, better, interpretative schemata to help us better understand what we see, hear, and read. Dewey doesn't offer us interpretative schemata, but he raises questions that help us think about and reflect on students' developing educational interests. In particular, he frames questions about understanding the logical and objective side of experience or the curriculum (EW 5: 173–174). Table 11.2 is an illustration of a few of the questions he thinks we might consider asking

Table 11.2   Understanding Students Through the Formal and Informal Curriculum:
An Interpretative Scheme

Question	Activity	Interest or Concern
What is the meaning of this behavior?	Writing verses for the teacher	Language learning? emotional development?
Is this her usual way of answering questions?	Jokingly making an insightful observation	Awkwardness in social settings?
What does this free activity suggest?	Playing with manipulatives	An interest in mathematics?
What do these questions imply?	Asking about the components of a hard drive	
How much does she value this activity or subject?	Talking at lunch about a visit to the local zoo	
Are there particular impulses, desires, or purposes behind this interest?	Offering to stay after school to assist the teacher	
Which of her abilities is she using in this project?	Volunteering to oversee the collection for a food drive	
Is this conversation related to the feelings her parents mentioned?	Arguing about the fairness of affirmative action	
What does this choice indicate?	Taking a course in art	
What is there about this experience that really appeals to her?		
Why does her response take this form rather than another?		
Why did she get upset?		
Where is her focus?		
What does this rejection intimate?		
Why does this appeal to her?		
What does her frown indicate?		
Does this have a long-term or short-term appeal?		

about specific activities of students and what they may indicate about students' interests, concerns, and development.

Of course, Table 11.2 is only one possible representation of Dewey's thinking, and it does not extend his thinking to the use of what the teacher learns about a student. In addition, some cells in Table 11.2 are empty for the purpose of stimulating thoughts about the questions, activities, and interests or concerns. If the figure stimulates a desire to create a more useful way of studying students, that would be consistent with Dewey's perspective, too.

A SUMMATIVE EXERCISE

Chapter 11   The Teacher as Wise Physician

Understandings	Qualities	Activities

READINGS

"The Meaning of Purpose," in *Experience and Education* (LW 13: 43–47).
"The Psychological Aspect of the School Curriculum," (EW 5: 164–176).
"Psychology in High-Schools from the Standpoint of the College," (EW 1: 81–89).
"The School and the Life of the Child," in *The School and Society* (MW 1: 21–38).

TWELVE

The Teacher as Builder

Teachers who are to be mediators of experience in relation to the personality growth of children or adults, must themselves be exceptionally well educated. It will not suffice to understand one age level .... It will not suffice to understand one subject .... The teachers of a free society will be continuous curriculum-builders, using the stuff and forms of community life and relating all of this to the developing needs of a group of learners who are thoroughly understood.

—John Dewey (LW 11: 544)

I n the two preceding chapters, we saw the place of students' experiences and purposes in education. Understanding them and acting on this knowledge is paramount, for the teacher cannot be either truly educative or artistic without doing such. Acting on these ideas, of course, is more challenging than understanding them. But the abilities of the teacher as a composer of student experiences and as a wise physician of their inner lives are necessarily called into action if she is going to be a builder. In this chapter,

Authors' Note: References to works by John Dewey are from the collection of his works published by Southern Illinois University Press: *The Early Works of John Dewey, 1882–1898; The Middle Works of John Dewey, 1899–1924;* and *The Later Works of John Dewey, 1925–1953.* References to these works are abbreviated as EW, MW, and LW, where, for example, EW 5: 94 indicates that the material cited or idea noted is in *The Early Works,* Volume 5, page 94.

we tie the ideas of student experience and purpose to the teacher as a twofold builder: a constructor of curricula and people. In part, this means that the teacher's composing educative experiences is inseparable from her involvement as a builder of curricula or, in a sense, a curriculum for each student.

> ### A Reflective Opportunity
>
> What possible dangers do you see in the idea of constructing people? Is it a risk worth taking by reflective teachers?

Plus, it suggests that as she uses her knowledge of students' minds, she is better able to create an environment that is filled with artistry and educative experiences. Her knowledge and artistry, therefore, play a role in her becoming involved in what Dewey terms "the greatest of all constructions—the building of a free and powerful character" (Archambault, 1964, p. 198). Luckily, the teacher builds independent personalities as she builds educative curricula. Hence, these two construction projects are interrelated and commingled, although we distinguish them for convenience and clarity. In Chapter 13, we shall see the teacher is a builder in a third sense: as a builder of classroom and school communities. All three construction projects overlap.

Before going into the realms of constructing curricula and people, we would like to examine a few ideas in the opening epigraph, which is from Dewey and Goodwin Watson's chapter, "The Forward View: A Free Teacher in a Free Society," originally published in *The Teacher and Society* (1937). Mining this quote reveals several nuggets, including recognizing that the teacher is or should be

- involved in a relationship of mediating students and experiences,
- concerned with students' personality development,
- informed about child and adolescent growth,
- prepared to teach more than one subject,
- characterized by building a curriculum that emerges from her prior studies and growing awareness of community life, and
- distinguished by a thorough understanding of the developmental needs of students.

Complementary nuggets can be found scattered elsewhere in Dewey's writings, as can a rationale for these ideas or prescriptions. We should not think, therefore, that these statements are either a complete statement of Dewey's views or that his claims are baseless. In reality, we are fortunate that the elliptical information reveals a partial rationale for Dewey and Watson's thinking. They think that the teacher needs to

- know the conception-through-Grade-12 development of children and youth, because students have to be understood in terms of their prior growth and lives, not merely in terms of their current grade-level characteristics;
- make decisions in the light of the student's past and present life, not just in terms of present interests and experiences; and
- offer insight into a full range of human experience in the classroom, not just one subject.

No doubt we may want to argue with Dewey and Watson about some of their ideas. That's good, because intellectual artists don't necessarily believe whatever they read. We might even start questioning his idea that we are in the business of personality development. Can we legitimately be involved when most of us are probably not psychologists or therapists? Or does Dewey mean only that we should be engaged in the social and psychological growth of our students? We may also wonder if it isn't asking too much of us when he claims that we should be able to offer insight into the whole of human experience? Does he expect us to know everything or merely express an informed judgment sometimes outside of our specialties?

Rather than pursuing these questions directly, let's begin looking at two building projects. First, we will examine curriculum construction. We will recall that Dewey believes that the interaction of the student with her environment is not only important but essential: It is demanded by both human nature and the nature of communities. The student's impulses, desires, and purposes make her an active, interacting person. In social settings, she interacts with other active people who have their own interests. These interactions need not be healthy ones and, therefore, ought to be guided initially by families, communities, schools, and others. Healthy personalities and communities may be natural, but they don't happen spontaneously. For this reason, we need environment and curriculum builders—mediators of experience—who are perceptive, wise artists who are capable of understanding individual and group needs.

Building an educative environment at school—or anywhere else—entails having a great deal of knowledge. This knowledge is partly identified in the opening epigraph, as was just noted. Supplementary knowledge was mentioned when we looked at Dewey's notion of the sources of a science of education and the teacher as wise physician. Every teacher, too, knows of many other resources that contribute to an educative environment, for example, a rich school library, a first-rate technological setting, well-equipped language and science laboratories, and modern physical and health facilities.

An Introspective Moment

Have you ever spent any time studying a student's neighborhood? talking with her family? observing her in typical out-of-school settings? Have you used the student's broader educational environment to facilitate in-school learning? What could you do to extend your abilities in this realm?

These sources of knowledge and curriculum development are fine, but we don't want to forget the words "the stuff and forms of community life" (LW 11: 544). City halls, jails, museums, ghettos, parks, hospitals, public housing, theaters, affluent enclaves, galleries, and banks, as well as government, civic, social, religious, and business centers, contribute to the "stuff and forms" of life. We may not wish to expose students to some of these sources of learning, for we may prefer to keep our curriculum sanitized, avoid certain realities, and promote others. Dewey wishes to keep both the curriculum and the environment simplified so that they do not overwhelm students, and he also says we should eliminate unworthy and inappropriate elements from the environment. He encourages us, too, to realize that the student's educational environment is not merely that which is in her visual and auditory fields, namely the classroom and school. In fact, if we are terribly unlucky, the student's educational environment and curriculum could be completely beyond the classroom and school. The educational environment that has her attention may be galleries, theaters, and museums—or street corners, drugs, and prisons.

Dewey's point in this discussion about the environment is that whatever enters the mind of the student while she is at school is her educational environment, even if it is in another neighborhood, city, country, hemisphere, or galaxy. Understanding that a student's educational environment is not necessarily the classroom is another reason for studying the mind of every student and for building a compelling educational environment in our schools: The student isn't involved in our curriculum if she is visiting a mall, arcade, or beach.

Could there be another curriculum builder in the classroom other than the teacher? The student is the obvious answer. She participates in forming the curriculum from different angles. She is, for joy or grief, a major contributor in our classrooms. At her best, she joins us as an edifying teacher of the teacher and her classmates. At her worst, she is a damaging or, at a minimum, distracting teacher of the teacher and her classmates. She and her friends are the curriculum in every classroom on occasions. They become *the* curriculum when they seek to influence or control a classroom.

That the environment or curriculum can be either positive and constructive or negative and destructive is obvious to Dewey. Recognizing this may explain why he thinks that although difficulties or obstacles are required ingredients for the stimulation of thought, not all obstacles "call out thinking" and some may "overwhelm and submerge and discourage" students (MW 9: 163). ➝His response is to build a learning environment or curriculum that is grounded in but leads beyond the purposes and life of each student. This, of course, isn't easy. Among other things the teacher must do, she has to be a reflective and assertive curriculum builder, incorporating the students, their backgrounds, and their immediate environments as positive forces and sources for learning, while not yielding control to them or accepting all they offer uncritically.

To do what Dewey suggests, the teacher must understand the dynamic interaction of the student and her educational environment, including the social dimensions (usually the teacher and other students, but ideally also parents and members of the external community) and the physical ones (all nonhuman elements). Consider a diagram we call the Student's Cycle of Environmental Interaction. We could also label this figure Steps in Problem Solving. Regrettably, Figure 12.1 seems to imply that each aspect is discrete and linear, which is not the case. Of course, multiple attempts at problem solving may be going on simultaneously and nearly all the time. Still, the cycle, we can say, is usually begun with activity as the student pursues her purposes or, less desirably, is stirred by impulses or desires.

This cycle, of course, includes the purposes and experiences of the student that enter into an activity. The center of the student's world is her current interests: her impulses, desires, or purposes. Dewey believes that in the ideal situation, the student is active in her physical and social environment as she learns. As she pursues her purposes through activities that the teacher has

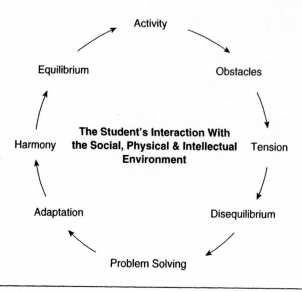

Figure 12.1   The Student's Cycle of Environmental Interaction

designed or created, she regularly encounters obstacles or problems, and these produce, among other things, tension. The tension, if sufficiently strong, results in an inner disequilibrium for the student. Because it is common to dislike disorder, the student then begins thinking or attempting to solve the problem. When thinking is successful, it leads the student to adapt or adjust or surmount the obstacle on her way to achieve her purposes. When the process is successful, inner harmony returns, and the student enjoys a temporary equilibrium. Shortly, however, the student reenters the cycle as she focuses on a new or, perhaps, old purpose and pursues it. This purpose may lead into a carefully designed experience or a thoughtfully allowed one, the latter kind providing more freedom for the student to pursue emerging or unexpected but valuable educational excursions. Thinking, then, is an attempt to solve a recognized problem. An important part of thinking may be understanding exactly what the problem is, not just blindly trying to answer questions. What is true of the planned learning experience in school is also true of the unplanned thinking of everyday life.

If we have taught or are a student of teaching, we know the situation is a great deal more complicated than we have described for at least two reasons. First, it seems likely that the student is often multitasking or multipurposing as she learns and that one of her tasks may reduce the efficiency of another one. The student also is probably prone to enter, exit, and reenter the cycle at different stages and after encounters with more than one obstacle. She might, for instance, encounter tension with one purpose and retreat to another school task or abandon the first task permanently. Or her disequilibrium may be suppressed during a class and return in another class or during the evening. The problem solving desired in one course or experience may actually occur in another class or on the way to school the next day. The student may return to school the next day, then, not with an obstacle, tension, or disequilibrium but with satisfaction, because she learned how to adapt to the obstacle after dinner. If we think of Dewey's thoughts about *an* experience and aesthetic experience, a successful progression through the cycle becomes *an* experience, and completion makes it an aesthetic experience, involving excitement, satisfaction, and fulfillment for the student and teacher. What completes it as *an* experience and gives it aesthetic value is what makes it educational: A problem is solved.

Consequently, Dewey says:

> In fact, in an experience of thinking, premises emerge only as a conclusion becomes manifest. The experience, like that of watching a storm reach its height and gradually subside, is one of continuous movement of subject-matters. Like the ocean in the storm, there are a series of waves; suggestions reaching out and being broken in a clash, or being carried onwards by a cooperative wave. If a conclusion is reached, it is that of a movement of anticipation and cumulation, one that finally comes to completion. A "conclusion" is no separate and independent thing; it is the consummation of a movement. (LW 10: 44–45)

Second, classroom realities make the situation more complicated and difficult than described. Consider a classroom of 30 students who are multitasking and multipurposing. Or, if we wish to get closer to bona fide classrooms, think of 10 students moved by their impulses, another 10 motivated by their desires, and another 10 deeply engaged in educative purposes and activities. The challenge of keeping up with this many intellectually shifting minds is mind boggling, demanding a teacher who is so well prepared that she can forget about information, facts, and interpretations so she can focus on the thinking of students. No wonder Dewey speaks of the teacher as an orchestral conductor and claims

> the art of giving shape to human powers and adapting them to social service is
> the supreme art; one calling into its service the best of artists; that no insight,
> sympathy, tact, executive power, is too great for such service. (EW 5: 94)

For those who really teach, it is easy to conclude with him that teaching
is "the most difficult and the most important of all human arts" (LW 3: 268).
Happily, we are aided in our artistry by a number of positive factors, including
the power of ideas once they are encountered by students:

> There is no mistake more common in schools than ignoring the self-
> propelling power of an idea. Once it is aroused, an alert mind fairly races
> along with it. Of itself it carries the student into new fields; it branches out
> into new ideas as a plant sends forth new shoots. (LW 8: 334)

Think back to the teacher as navigator and recall that the student supplies
the energy for her voyage. We can now add to the student's energy the complementary energy of ideas. Ideas lack energy, however, if they are devoid
of the human and social issues. If we stick to a diet of remote, dry, safe
thoughts—ideas suffering from anorexia—we can expect sickly and dying
classrooms. Active students need lively ideas, or they will create their own
curriculum and escape to another part of their far-flung environment.

Builders of people, too? This idea isn't popular for some folks. But
Dewey does not measure responsibilities by popularity. We can—and
should—argue with him about the notion and its features, but it seems unlikely
that he would change his mind. As usual, however, it is worth understanding
his position a little better so we'll know why we are objecting to his idea if we
are. So, let's get a little more clear about what he means by the phrase "the
greatest of all constructions—the building of a free and powerful character"
(Archambault, 1964, p. 198). Although we have encountered similar ideas
before, the word *character* might trouble us more than the other ones; but this
does not mean the other ideas are innocent bystanders. Of character, he says
that it means "a measure of mental power, mastery of truths and laws, love of
beauty in nature and art, strong human sympathy, and unswerving moral rec-
titude" (Archambault, 1964, p. 197). Often, we want many or all of these qualities in our spouses, friends, supervisors, stockbrokers, and politicians. But this
doesn't mean we want them in our students or, more important, think we
should cultivate their acquisition. Or does it? Interestingly, Dewey implies that
human sympathy is "the cardinal requisite" of the teacher, because it involves

caring for "human life and its aspirations" (Archambault, 1964, p. 199). Perhaps it will only cloud the picture to add that Dewey thinks the building of a learning atmosphere and people is a single enterprise that is inescapably moral and value laden. Does it help to realize that part of his ethical theory includes attending to the interests of others and developing reflective citizens and healthy communities?

QUOTES AND QUESTIONS

We may be able to tie together Dewey's ideas by looking at what he says about crafting or composing problems for students. First, he advises us that the obstacles, difficulties, or problems that students encounter in school should be carefully selected to ensure that they are a part of the student's world, not ones that are artificially created by us. This means, then, that "the giving of problems, the putting of questions, the assigning of tasks, the magnifying of difficulties" ought to meet criteria:

> (a) Is there anything but a problem? Does the question naturally suggest itself within some situation or personal experience? Or is it an aloof thing, a problem only for the purposes of conveying instruction in some school topic? Is it the sort of trying that would arouse observation and engage experimentation outside of school? (b) Is it the pupil's own problem, or is it the teacher's or textbook's problem, made a problem for the pupil only because he cannot get the required mark or be promoted or win the teacher's approval, unless he deals with it? (MW 9: 161–162)

How often do school assignments, questions, problems, and tasks with which you are most familiar meet Dewey's standards? Should they? Although the problem may seem real enough to a student, does it have educational potential?

Second, obstacles and problems have to be carefully crafted to ensure that they do not overpower students. Are the problems reasonably familiar, adequately challenging, and appropriately confusing? Once again, the art of teaching is on his mind:

> A large part of the art of instruction lies in making the difficulty of new problems large enough to challenge thought, and small enough so that, in addition to the confusion naturally attending the novel elements, there shall be luminous familiar spots from which helpful suggestions may spring. (MW 9: 163–164)

Do you think we should supplement Dewey's thought with the idea that another important part of the art of instruction is recognizing when activities are too demanding and then reconceptualizing them? Is this a problem with which experienced teachers can assist new teachers? Moreover, how do we ensure that students see the value of what they achieve, and, at least implicitly, that they have moved from blind impulse to a thought-out purpose? That they are developing higher-order, reflective skills?

When we are creative teachers, we sometimes incur the displeasure of parents, colleagues, and supervisors, because we build environments and students that no longer exactly fit a cultural mold. The impossible challenge is to be both creative and compliant. Dewey advises, directly in one case and indirectly in the other, both the inventive teacher and the helpful supervisor:

> A good deal of supervision . . . seems to have a great deal of "super" in it and not much of "vision." It is the business of the supervisor to look over the field, to get a larger, wider, more thorough view of it than the conditions of the classroom teacher can permit. It is the privilege of the supervisor and directing officer to give the classroom teacher the benefit of this larger, more comprehensive vision of the field. (MW 15: 186)

The whole effect of organized administration sometimes seems to force a kind of standardization that is unfavorable to the development of the teacher's individuality and to the teacher's cooperating in the development of the pupil's individuality (MW 15: 181).

What implicit and explicit advice do you see for the supervisor in these comments? The teacher? What advice would you add for each?

IMPLICATIONS FOR THE TEACHER

Nothing, then, could be further from the truth than the sometimes-heard claim that Dewey argues that we should leave students to follow their own interests, whatever they might be and wherever they might lead. In his philosophy of teaching, the teacher builds or develops (a) an environment that draws students to activities that will lead to educative experiences, and (b) an understanding of how to identify and address problems. He expects us to build strong students by leading them from impulses to purposes and from anesthetic experiences to aesthetic ones. Moreover, he expects us to cultivate independent thinkers by leading students from their personal knowledge into organized forms of knowledge, respecting and using the former while seeking the latter. To pursue these responsibilities successfully means that the teacher will sometimes be on the edge of what a supervisor, administrator, district, parent, or community believes is only tolerable. The younger the students we teach, the less freedom we may have as we build curricula and people. The more social and human controversies in our teaching field, the greater the danger of irritating someone. The

> ### A Teacher Snapshot
>
> Do you know a teacher who is extraordinarily good at dealing with exciting and sensitive ideas? Why is she so good? Do you know other teachers who are less successful in dealing with the same issues? What characteristics or conditions do they lack that the first teacher has?

younger we are, the less inhibited we may be about introducing controversial issues but the more vulnerable we are to community pressure, because we do not yet have a fund of relevant experience and are not yet established and a well-known quantity. But we can encounter trouble with any age group, in any teaching field, and at any age.

Several other implications of being a builder can be seen below the surface of our discussions. First, we need to remember that exciting ideas are great stimulants for growth and that they constitute an important part of the environment to be constructed. Experience with these ideas by students is enabled by the teacher as she gets inside them, sees them as her students do, and determines the points of contact they make with her students' lives. In part, this means that—as we saw in the last chapter—we have to imaginatively enter the students' experiences as wise physicians who probe their innermost interests and capabilities (MW 9: 8–9). Second, students need to address genuine problems with their lively ideas if we as teachers are going to keep them engaged in educative activities and growing. Third, the wise mother offers us insight. She knows how far to lead her children into previously uncharted waters and when they are close to being overwhelmed. Her first concern is with building her children as people, not for the ideological trends that she loves to debate with neighbors and colleagues at the office. She listens to experts (her colleagues who understand the setting) and her own experience (her interactions with others and their consequences) and can go about her responsibilities with confidence and conviction. Fourth, there are some teaching opportunities or situations that are too sensitive for one teacher, but not for others. Wisdom suggests that we need to look for schools that allow us to feel reasonably comfortable. Professional stimulation is one thing; constantly being under great professional stress isn't wise or likely to help us make contributions to children and society. Moreover, we seem to gain little by receiving a letter of termination and opening the door for a more compliant replacement. Fifth, although the artistic teacher, like any artist, can make mistakes, the joys of teaching and of seeing students learn and grow need to be experienced on a regular basis. Seeing them develop into independent thinkers who choose for themselves but act on behalf of others is also something we need to observe on a regular basis. If we are not habitually building students because of political and social issues, then we need to find a new studio, ideally one that appreciates artistry and aesthetic experience but at least one that tolerates them.

As we close this discussion with a sixth implication, we do so by raising a set of questions about the teacher as a builder. Think for a moment about the ways we assist in building an environment and people. Which dimension or dimensions of the learning environment consume most of your time? Is it the physical space? Or do the technology, supplies, and materials take up most of your time? What about the social and emotional elements? Do they get much attention? How much consideration is given to planning experiences that will occur in a democratic atmosphere? What adjustments do you need to make to develop into a better-balanced builder?

Now, let's pause for a related building project. How much do you think about being a co-builder of people? Does the idea seem a little scary? Is building an environment related to building people? Do the well-built elements of the environment suggest that students will similarly be hearty in the same areas? If you consider yourself a co-builder, where is most of your time devoted? Is it to intellectual matters? emotional development? physical maturation? moral enhancement? social progress? volitional growth? and so forth? Is the whole student usually developed in your classes, or are certain features neglected?

A SUMMATIVE EXERCISE

Chapter 12   The Teacher as Builder

Understandings	Qualities	Activities

READINGS

"The Forward View: A Free Teacher in a Free Society," (LW 11: 535–547).

"The Live Creature," in *Art as Experience* (LW 10: 9–25).

"Thinking in Education," in *Democracy and Education* (MW 9: 159–170).

"What Psychology Can Do for the Teacher." (1964). In R. Archambault (Ed.), *John Dewey on education* (pp. 195–211). Chicago: University of Chicago Press.

THIRTEEN

The Teacher as Leader

The older type of instruction tended to treat the teacher as a dictatorial ruler. The newer type sometimes treats the teacher as a negligible fact, almost as an evil, though a necessary one. In reality the teacher is the intellectual leader of a social group. He is a leader, not in virtue of official position, but because of wider and deeper knowledge and matured experience. The supposition that the principle of freedom confers liberty upon the pupils, but that the teacher is outside of its range and must abdicate all leadership is merely silly.

—John Dewey (LW 8: 337)

Given the ideologies that swirl in educational circles, it is easy to want to draw the conclusion that teachers are either dictators or negligible factors. For example, if we are truly bright and reflective teachers, we know that we have to direct, push, drag, and tell students exactly what to do to get

---

Authors' Note: References to works by John Dewey are from the collection of his works published by Southern Illinois University Press: *The Early Works of John Dewey, 1882–1898; The Middle Works of John Dewey, 1899–1924;* and *The Later Works of John Dewey, 1925–1953.* References to these works are abbreviated as EW, MW, and LW, where, for example, EW 5: 94 indicates that the material cited or idea noted is in *The Early Works,* Volume 5, page 94.

Table 13.1 Types of Counterproductive Thinking

Type of Thinking	Description
Dichotomous thinking	Thinking that assumes that the truth is only on one side of an argument and that an argument can only have two sides
Compromissorial thinking	Thinking that assumes that we must agree to bring together even inconsistent ideas so that all sides can work together
Ideological thinking	Thinking that assumes that one's ideology or "ism" includes and fairly accounts for the important truths there are to know
Reactive thinking	Thinking that is directed to and so controlled largely by opposing ideas that we dislike or reject
Gracious thinking	Thinking that generously accepts a worthless idea or theory that cannot be applied or practiced
Nostalgic thinking	Thinking that assumes that the past always provides the best answers to questions and the most defensible ideals
Dogmatic thinking	Thinking that refuses to reflect on or question its own basic beliefs

them to participate in the activities that lead to the learning outcomes prescribed by the school and district. Our critics may refer to us as dictators of the powerless, but we know that we are wiser than they are and are doing what is in the best interest of immature children and youth. On the other hand, there is another perspective that says if we are genuinely intelligent and caring teachers, we recognize that we should merely open the universe to students and allow them to discover, create, and construct on their own. Our critics may call us facilitators of angelic whims, if not largely passive playground supervisors, but we know that we are wiser than they are and are doing what is in the best interest of maturing children and youth.

If we represent a third group of brilliant and discerning educators, we know it won't do any good to try to change the minds of the educational dictators or pedagogical facilitators who have just spoken. They are too dogmatic, idealistic, or naïve. Most are hopelessly pigheaded, so we'll just leave them to their pedagogical poison and get on with our jobs! We can simply ignore these idiots. We know how to teach without getting involved in these ideological controversies.

Either-or thinking—the dictator versus the facilitator—greatly troubles Dewey. He sees this type of thinking so often that he concludes the entire human race is inclined

> to think in terms of extreme opposites. It is given to formulating beliefs in terms of *Either-Ors*, between which it recognizes no intermediate possibilities. When forced to recognize that the extremes cannot be acted upon, it is still inclined to hold that they are all right in theory but that when it comes to practical matters circumstances compel us to comprise. (LW 13: 5)

In *Experience and Education*, Dewey amplifies his objections to either-or or dichotomous thinking along with other kinds of thinking that are self-defeating. Unproductive thinking, he argues, should be avoided if we want to think clearly and comprehensively about education and other matters (LW 13: 3–10). These types of thinking are summarized in Table 13.1.

Understanding these kinds of thinking and what makes them problematic and unproductive is particularly important for the teacher as an

---

An Introspective Moment

Can you remember a recent occasion when you engaged in counterproductive thinking? Did anyone notice?

"intellectual leader" in committee with colleagues, in public with community members, but especially in the classroom with children or youth (LW 8: 337). If we engage in these types of thinking, we are unlikely to get things right, and our model will influence our students to think similarly and thereby promote (a) having one-sided viewpoints, (b) synthesizing contradictory beliefs, (c) being closed minded about others' ideas, (d) having knee-jerk responses to opponents, (e) accepting unwarranted conclusions, (f) romanticizing the past, and (g) privileging our own beliefs. Some of our students will probably, like us, favor some kinds of thinking more than others, but it is remarkable how we can practice all types of reasoning. Classroom leaders, however, should become increasingly aware of their own and others' unproductive ways of thinking and seek to nurture reflective inquiry by all.

Dewey goes farther down the unproductive thinking road in *The Child and the Curriculum* (1902, MW 2: 271ff). When we disagree about how to solve a problem, he suggests that the path to reflective thinking has its temptations. We may

- find it easy to stick to our current opinions, rather than rethink them;
- look for ways to support our ideas, rather than consider the merits of the arguments against our ideas;
- select the point of view that appeals most to us, rather than determining if the attractive ideas are based on a reflective examination of relevant factors;
- cling to a single idea or variable in such a manner that we distort the larger picture;
- decide to accept everyone's ideas because we are weary of arguing and reasoning; and
- go on with conflicting opinions because we consider the disagreement insoluble and action of some sort necessary.

The path that Dewey encourages us to follow is indirectly implied by the problems in the counterproductive thinking he discourages, but also when he suggests that when we reach an impasse in solving a dispute we—at least in an effort to learn more about the views of those with whom we disagree—intentionally (a) back away from the fixed meanings of terms that we use, (b) use words that are less ideologically rooted, (c) examine issues through the lenses of others, (d) set aside our present ideas as we study issues, and (e) reconsider the facts we believe to be true (MW 2: 271–291).

> **A Teacher Snapshot**
>
> Who was the best intellectual leader who ever guided your thinking? Can you list several of her tendencies or qualities as a thinker? What particular traits or habits did you especially admire?

Making these five decisions is not the same thing as being absolutely neutral about facts and interpretations. Nor is it claiming that we are completely objective. Neither neutrality nor objectivity is possible as an absolute attainment. Plus, when we use the lenses of others to look for and at facts and their meanings, we are intentionally trying to see through another interpretative framework, not from a noninterpretative or neutral one. Of course, degrees of objectivity (MW 7: 10; LW 5: 58) are sometimes possible and pedagogically useful too, but education itself can be neither neutral nor indifferent to a variety of matters (LW 8: 80–81). What Dewey encourages is a degree of separation from our emotional and intellectual ties so that we can begin to see beyond the limits of our perspective and grow in our understanding, bringing people closer together conceptually, intellectually, politically, and socially. That is, he wants us and our students to become open-minded: to cultivate and practice an "alert curiosity and spontaneous outreaching" and

> an active desire to listen to more sides than one; to give heed to facts from whatever source they come; to give full attention to alternative possibilities; to recognize the possibility of error even in beliefs that are dearest to us. (LW 8: 136)

Believing this, as he does, it is easy to see why he argues that reflective thinking helps to "emancipate us from merely impulsive and merely routine activity" (LW 8: 125).

Being open-minded and learning to think outside of our intellectual gullies has many implications for the artistic teacher. The art of teaching, as we already know, includes the "art of thinking" (LW 1: 287), and the art of thinking involves "the art of questioning" (LW 8: 331). The person who is growing in her open-mindedness enjoys the benefits of practicing the arts of thinking and questioning. This is the case because "thinking is inquiry, investigation, turning over, probing or delving into, so as to find something new or to see what is already known in a different light. In short, it is *questioning*" (LW 8: 330). Of the art of questioning, Dewey says there are several ideas that we can keep in mind. Specifically, good questions

- develop students' reflection by getting them to use the information, ideas, and theories they already understand to solve new problems;
- focus students' attention on subjects or issues, not on guessing what the teacher's opinion is;
- direct students' inquiry to the broader topic or problem rather than narrow and dead-end queries;
- stimulate students' thinking to review entire sets of ideas so that they understand the significance and context of what they have learned; and
- heighten students' expectations by engendering a degree of suspense about new and future threads of thought about the material and ideas investigated.

Teaching, thinking, and questioning, therefore, go together in the theory and practice of the artistic teacher. Engaging in and fostering these activities undermines dictatorial tendencies and provides cogent evidence that the teacher who thinks reflectively isn't a negligible factor. Nor is she someone who walks away from controversies because they are frustrating and sometimes stimulated by people who merely enjoy arguing or irritating others. Instead, she takes away from discussions and arguments the best supported ideas she hears.

QUOTES AND QUESTIONS

Dewey frequently defends an active role for the teacher in the classroom and attacks the notion that she is merely a facilitator of the wishes of students. Often he defends the active role in the ways he portrays the teacher, for instance, as leader, gardener, physician, navigator, artist, engineer, mother, pioneer, and builder. Believing that these kinds of people are inactive, passive, or insignificant is difficult if not impossible. Behind these images is a series of arguments that provide a rationale for his beliefs. Among these arguments is a moral or ethical one that the teacher has no right to discard what she has learned from experience or formal studies. She isn't justified in hoarding what she knows. Others, especially her students, deserve the opportunity to learn what she has learned. To refrain from being actively involved in the guidance of classroom activities and the sharing of relevant information, Dewey believes, constitutes a twofold disloyalty to the very idea of learning. He sums up these two betrayals:

> The educator is false to the understanding that he should have obtained from his own past experience [e.g., that past experience is educative and valuable when reflected on]. He is also unfaithful to the fact that all human experience is ultimately social: that it involves contact and communication. The mature person, to put it in moral terms, has no right to withhold from the young on given occasions whatever capacity for sympathetic understanding his own experience has given him. (LW 13: 21)

Dewey's thinking, at least to a degree, is shaped by the idea that the teacher is not only an intellectual in the classroom but also a moral leader in the learning community that emerges in the classroom. "The teacher loses the position of external boss or dictator but takes on that of leader of group activities" (LW 13: 37). He likewise believes that the activities that the teacher selects for the classroom community are "the chief carrier of control" or what we would call classroom management (LW 13: 35). We can add to our previously developed picture of the teacher as builder, therefore, an additional thought: The teacher not only builds curricula and people but a classroom community. In many ways, the three are inseparable: The life of the classroom group or community *is* part of the curriculum and a fundamental way of assisting in the building of each student as a person. So the teacher as an intellectual and moral leader and "a member of the community" has at least two distinct responsibilities: "to select the influences which shall affect the child [or youth] and to assist him in properly responding to these influences" (EW 5: 88). Unless a community is built that embraces the teacher as a member, education is "reduced to a pressure from without" (EW 5: 85). A pedagogical artist, then, works to become a member of the class social group and continues to work from within as she leads the group.

> **An Introspective Moment**
>
> What kinds of challenges have you experienced with classroom management? What approaches to management seem to work well for you? Have you been able to nurture a classroom community? In what ways, if any, did the classroom community management affect group interactions?

Dewey anticipates objections, including the possibility that an active teacher will impose activities and experiences on students:

> In some schools the tendency to minimize the place of the teacher takes the form of supposing that it is an arbitrary imposition for the teacher to propose the line of work to be followed or to arrange the situation within which problems and topics arise. It is held that . . . all suggestions are to come from . . . [students]. Especially has this idea been applied in some kindergartens and primary grades. The result is often that described in the story of a young child who, on arriving at school, said to the teacher: "Do we have to do to-day what we want to do?" (LW 8: 337)

But we would hardly expect Dewey to favor arbitrary imposition, and he immediately adds:

> The alternative to proposals by the teacher is that the suggestions of things to do come [1] from chance, [2] from casual contacts, [3] from what the child saw on his way to school, what he did yesterday, what he sees the next child doing, etc. Since the purpose to be carried out must come, directly or indirectly, from somewhere in the environment, denial to the teacher of the power to propose it merely substitutes accidental contact with some other person or scene for the intelligent planning of the very individual who, if he has a right to be a teacher at all, has the best knowledge of the needs and possibilities of the members of the group of which he is a part. (LW 8: 337–338)

What are we to make of Dewey's claims? How active can the teacher be if at the same time she does not impose herself and her values on students? Does he exaggerate when he says that we have a moral responsibility to share what we have learned with students? In what sense, if at all, can we agree that we are community builders in our classrooms, especially if the community meant is one that extends beyond the classroom and school? If we build classroom communities, will they solve management problems? Don't neighborhood communities have problems? Or do we live in neighborhoods but not communities? In another vein, we ask, do we really have "the best knowledge of the needs and possibilities" of our students (LW 8: 338)? Are there others who better understand the educational needs and potentialities of our students? Should we really become members of a classroom community with our students? Do we need to keep a distance between students and us?

IMPLICATIONS FOR THE TEACHER

When we decided to become teachers, we may not have aspired to become intellectual, moral, and group leaders; build classroom communities; and engage in the art of thinking. The thought of leading students to think for themselves may have been mentioned to us, but we might not have paid much attention to the idea. We may wonder if some focused study on leading students to think would be appropriate if we are supposed to exhibit as well as cultivate the art of thinking. And how will we, we may muse, consciously integrate reflection in our classrooms, especially in settings in which thinking is not only not valued but explicitly discouraged?

Community building wasn't in our curriculum, either. What are the implications of the idea of community building? Is it possible in our schools? Can we build communities if students change teachers every hour or so? Should we also think about developing a community or communities in our schools, not just in our classrooms? Where do we begin? Can we build communities given everything else we have to do? How do we get on the inside of a class community and guide it from within? And what is the difference between a community and a clique? or a gang? or a group of friends?

Beyond the implications these questions suggest, there are others that also emerge. First, any human art related to teaching, whether thinking or questioning, needs to be studied and practiced. Reading and discussing these activities with our classmates or colleagues seems a good place to begin. Practicing what we learn with feedback from classmates or colleagues seems well advised, too. Second, if Dewey is right, the building of a community is worth our energy and time. He sees a community making major contributions to our success in the areas of classroom management, character development, and educative experiences—as well as a method of teaching, as we shall see in the next chapter. Students learn more of what they need to learn if the community is a genuine learning community. This suggests that we probably need to study community building, too. Where can we look for helpful literature and ideas on this subject? Third, we may need to analyze the concepts of imposition and education in more depth. The tension that exists in attempting to prevent the former and to foster the latter is worth understanding better. For example, if imposition is in part attempting to force on students ideas or behavior in an unwarranted manner and education is in part seeking to cultivate thinking and growth in a defensible fashion, then we may have a beginning point for distinguishing impositional and educational undertakings.

Let's change directions as we examine implications. What do we think of our own development as a class or group leader? Do we need to lead more or less in most activities? Are we prone to be too directive? Or are we inclined to neglect our leadership responsibilities? What is the most challenging part of leading for us? If we allow time for free activity, are we leading?

Reminding ourselves of the background of our epigraph is worth doing as we close. In context, Dewey says we should be leaders in social groups or in our classes. The leadership is intellectual in nature. No doubt, serving as leaders in other ways is important at times, but being an intellectual leader is indispensable for the teacher. For Dewey, it is founded on two considerations: our richer knowledge and richer experience. The knowledge should be obvious by our depth of understanding of student needs and abilities, grasp of subject matter, comprehension of professional knowledge, study of collateral subjects, and preparation of daily lessons (LW 8: 338–339). As we prepare to become better educated and as we reflect on our experiences, then, we are preparing to be leaders.

Elsewhere, Dewey clarifies what he thinks about our unofficial leadership and says it involves both intellectual and moral dimensions:

It is not merely leadership *in* education but it is leadership *by* education rather than by law and government authority. Indeed, it is a kind of leadership that gives a new meaning to the word. It is a process of guidance. It takes effect through inspiration, stimulation, communication of ideas, discovery and report of facts, rather than by decree. It is compelled to trust for the most part to the power of facts and ideas and to the willingness of the community at large to receive and act upon them. (LW 3: 252–253)

Building on the educational role of leaders, Dewey also tells us that leadership has "two sides" (LW 6: 128). Specifically, he claims:

There can be leadership as there can be following only when human beings think together about a common theme with a shared purpose to a common result. Leadership is absent because this power of collective thinking in connection with solidarity of emotion and desire is lacking today. We have in its stead attempts to whip up a seeming unity of idea and sentiment by means of catch-words, slogans, and advertising devices. Few persons, however, are fooled by them except possibly those engaged in promulgating them. (LW 6: 128)

We close with implications from this quotation. In our informal leadership roles, we can provide input into the lives of our schools by working toward common themes, purposes, and outcomes that serve students, staff, and society well. These themes, purposes, and outcomes, for Dewey, emerge from the practice of a democratic understanding of what schools should do. But agreement in these realms doesn't occur unless intellectual and moral leaders take the time—an odd but essential commitment of both formal and informal leaders—to think collectively through questions, issues, and options. We provide leadership, then, by learning, thinking, and meeting to share what we understand.

We also provide leadership when we bring the artistic spirit to discussions and are passionate and enthusiastic about the themes, purposes, and outcomes we agree on and pursue. In this kind of setting, we help build school and classroom environments that undermine the efforts of others who wish to impose a culture of clichés. Our greatest educational contribution as informal leaders, therefore, may be the cultivation of schools and classrooms that are built on the thinking of our colleagues and co-learners, students.

A SUMMATIVE EXERCISE

Chapter 13   The Teacher as Leader

Understandings	Qualities	Activities

READINGS

The Child and the Curriculum (MW 2: 271–291).
"The Recitation and the Training of Thought," in *How We Think* (LW 8: 327–341).
"Traditional vs. Progressive Education," in *Experience and Education* (LW 13: 5–10).

FOURTEEN

The Teacher as Classroom Teacher

Instruction always runs the risk of swamping the pupil's own vital, though narrow, experience under masses of communicated material. The mere instructor ceases and the vital teacher begins at the point where communicated matter stimulates into fuller and more significant life that which has entered by the straight and narrow gate of sense perception and motor activity. Genuine communication involves contagion; its name should not be taken in vain by terming communication that which produces no community of thought and purpose between the child and the race of which he is the heir.

—John Dewey (MW 6: 356)

As we noted earlier, teaching is like many other occupations and activities. Some similarities are actually intrinsic and vital parts of both

Authors' Note: References to works by John Dewey are from the collection of his works published by Southern Illinois University Press: *The Early Works of John Dewey, 1882–1898; The Middle Works of John Dewey, 1899–1924;* and *The Later Works of John Dewey, 1925–1953.* References to these works are abbreviated as EW, MW, and LW, where, for example, EW 5: 94 indicates that the material cited or idea noted is in *The Early Works,* Volume 5, page 94.

occupations and activities. Others offer one-of-a-kind insights into teaching, but the insights offered—although important—may not be fundamental or vital features of the work of the classroom teacher. But in combination, these similarities are invaluable in helping us better understand the science and art of teaching. Still, teaching is teaching and involves a unique set of activities. True, we are somewhat—perhaps a great deal—like pioneers, gardeners, and navigators, but we aren't full-fledged, literal pioneers, gardeners, and navigators. We are teachers. Images of teachers and teaching, therefore, may well capture vivid, dynamic, and compelling pictures for us, but they still leave out dimensions of the art that strangers to the profession frequently fail to appreciate even if they view teaching as including artistic and aesthetic elements. So the fact that teaching has both similarities to other intentionally directed endeavors and yet distinguishing responsibilities means we need to press on to get a more complete picture of the artistry of the teacher.

Classroom teacher? Yes, this concept may seem mundane and lack the luster of a creative chef, courageous pioneer, wise physician, orchestral conductor, or social engineer, but it is an honorable term and has the advantage of suggesting who we are and what we do regularly. In reality, we are classroom teachers unless we've joined the ranks of administrators or support personnel or have had our classes assigned to an auditorium, laboratory, or gymnasium. Or perhaps we have been assigned to a kitchen, storage room, or hallway. Whatever: We are primarily teachers who are concerned with the learning of students. We are still educators in the broader sense of building curricula, serving on committees, and attending staff development activities, but we do these other professional things because they help us be better professionals in the classroom.

Nearly everything we have examined thus far is indirectly or directly related to the classroom. But much has been circuitously developed or only suggested through understanding the student, curriculum, or environment. Now we wish to focus our attention to the classroom teacher as an artist. In the process of pursuing this understanding, we examine several questions: (1) What kind of attitude should characterize the classroom teacher as an artist? (2) What do we know about the method of the artistic classroom teacher? and (3) How do we evaluate the classroom success of an artist? Partial answers to these questions are scattered throughout the previous chapters. Now we will draw on these past ideas as well as complement them with new insights from Dewey. These three topics—the *attitude* of the artistic teacher, the *method* of the artistic teacher, and the *measure* of the artistic teacher—overlap and commingle in Dewey's thinking and writings.

As we begin with our first question, we will look at what Dewey says about the teacher or the artist's attitude. In *How We Think*, Dewey lays out some ideas on the artist's attitude and spirit. To begin, he connects the spirit or ideal attitude of the teacher to both the means and the ends of teaching. The former are "inspired by recognition of the [value and importance of the] end they serve" (LW 8: 348). To rephrase his thought, the teacher's attitude and spirit are determined not by what does happen later but by the importance she places on the growth she seeks for each student. The potential student outcomes inspire her as a person, professional, and artist. Her attitude and spirit are characterized by the loves we examined earlier: associating with students, communicating knowledge, playing with ideas, and arousing intellectual interests (LW 13: 344–345). These loves reveal a spirit that is sincere, passionate, caring, contagious, and powerful.

> **A Teacher Snapshot**
>
> Who better than anyone else best demonstrates what Dewey suggests by the artist's attitude and spirit? Is it easy to learn such an attitude? If not, how can we cultivate it?

In addition, the ideal spirit or attitude of the classroom artist exhibits a harmonious balance of "mental playfulness and seriousness," with the understanding that the former involves the latter (LW 8: 348):

> To give the mind this free play is not to encourage toying with a subject, but is to be interested in the unfolding of the subject on its own account, apart from any subservience to a preconceived belief or habitual aim. Mental play is open-mindedness, faith in the power of thought to preserve its own integrity without external supports and arbitrary restrictions. Hence free mental play involves seriousness, the earnest following of the development of subject matter. It is incompatible with carelessness or flippancy, for it exacts accurate noting of every result reached in order that every conclusion may be put to further use. (LW 8: 347)

The artistic classroom teacher's attitude, then, includes conveying to students the feeling that it is great to (a) play with intellectual and social issues, (b) wait to see what unfolds and is learned from later class inquiries, (c) speculate about what conclusions will emerge and ultimately be justified,

(d) look for applications of what is learned to present and future problems, and (e) wonder what might have happened if we had done differently. With the hand and heart of a classroom artist guiding educative experiences, the knowledge that comes from these playful ventures and inquiries becomes the grounds for further learning and action. No wonder Dewey talks of education in terms of continued growth and the capacity for continued growth, and education as giving people power. The goal of continued thinking and learning, then, inspires the means the teacher selects (LW 8: 348). The passion she has and spreads is a moving force in the classroom. As each student becomes absorbed in learning, "the subject carries him on" (LW 8: 137). Thus:

> Questions occur to him spontaneously; a flood of suggestions pour in on him; further inquiries and readings are indicated and followed; instead of having to use his energy to hold his mind to the subject . . . the material holds and buoys his mind up and gives an onward impetus to thinking. (LW 8: 137)

Our second question may seem to be a discrete idea, but we cannot ultimately separate the teacher's method from the attitude or spirit of the artist. Understanding Dewey's view of method isn't as easy as we might expect, for it involves comprehending a complex or set of ideas, especially three related methods: methods of teaching, methods of learning, and methods of thinking. In addition, it involves understanding what he labels the "generic and specific conditions" of the school and classroom (LW 8: 158), as well as "general and individual" methods (MW 9: 177). Buried in these ideas is what we may call "technique" or "method" (MW 9: 172). In all, we are interested in examining (a) the conditions of classrooms and schools; (b) the methods of thinking, learning, and teaching; and (c) the techniques of the teacher. These three domains, although distinguished for clearness and expediency, once again overlap at times. These ideas are summarized in Table 14.1, The Teacher's Methodology.

First, we turn to the conditions of classrooms and schools. As we begin our examination, we can't do better than read Dewey's *How We Think*, in which he candidly declares:

> The problem of *method* in forming habits of reflective thought is the problem establishing *conditions* that will arouse and guide curiosity; of setting up the connections in things experienced that will on later occasions promote the flow of *suggestions*, create problems and purposes that will favor *consecutiveness* in the succession of ideas. (LW 8: 157)

Table 14.1   The Teacher's Methodology

Type of Methodology	Description
Classroom and school conditions or environments	Classroom and school environments are methods of teaching
Specific conditions	Methods of teaching a specific subject
General methods	Methods that are intelligently directed toward ends, using the scientific method to think through how teaching and learning may be best achieved
Individual methods	Methods that are determined by the artistic style and individuality of the teacher to effectively teach each student

These words are crammed with Dewey's specific meanings: *method, habit, thought, problem, conditions, curiosity, connections, experience, suggestions,* and *consecutiveness.* One, *conditions,* is our immediate concern and is for Dewey an approximate synonym for the concept environment, an idea that we have already explored (LW 8: 158). Notice the contrast between educative and miseducative classroom conditions in Table 14.2 that emerges from Dewey's explication of classroom and school conditions.

Being cognizant of conditions, then, means the teacher recognizes that her method of teaching includes not just what she consciously designs but "anything in the atmosphere and conduct of the school that reacts in any way upon the curiosity, the responsiveness, and the orderly activity" of students (LW 8:157).

Dewey continues this line of reasoning by advocating an idea and practice that runs counter to the tendencies of pedagogical police everywhere: The teacher who understands both the minds of her students and the conditions of her school and classroom can be "trusted" to select "the *specific* conditions" or methods in the "narrower and more technical sense" that are related to teaching biology, reading, mathematics, music, and so on (LW 8: 158). In our teaching, however, we need to remember that the specific conditions or the methods that we select for teaching and learning a subject cannot completely or even largely overcome classroom and school conditions that are counterproductive. The conditions of the whole school can and do overwhelm the efforts of even expert artists scattered down its corridors in classrooms,

Table 14.2   A Contrast of Classroom Conditions: An Example

Educative Conditions	Miseducative Conditions
Students are asking questions	Students are quiet and passive
Students are engaged in exploratory activities	Student activity is seen as inconvenient and disruptive
Students make connections between words and things	Students memorize words and terms
Students anticipate the future through their plans and projects	Students activities are limited to thinking about present problems
Students indirectly learn to think by solving authentic problems	Students may be directly taught the steps of reflective thinking
Students learn new questions and issues as they solve existing problems	Students learn to solve artificially designed problems

laboratories, and auditoriums. So unless school and classroom cultures, environments, or conditions are carefully nurtured, we are going to have unusually difficult challenges as artists of human beliefs and behaviors. The problem of method, therefore, is to an extent one of community or culture building.

Dewey takes a much different approach to method in *Democracy and Education*, where he explains his ideas about general and individual methods of teaching (MW 9: 171–187). His philosophy of general methods is where we begin. We note that he believes "the method of teaching is the method of art, of action intelligently directed by ends" (MW 9: 177). This is his account of general methods. It means, among other things, that the teacher relies on neither "ready-made rules" nor "native gifts" (MW 9: 177). On the other hand, only a person practicing to be a fool would ignore the body of experiential information, the reflective tradition, and the research data about successful teaching. The artistic teacher simply does not yield to the temptations of (a) rigidly using this collective wisdom, reflection, and research (MW 9: 177) or (b) unconsciously losing her "emotional and imaginative perception" as she teaches (LW 10: 267).

A Reflective Opportunity

If you had to speculate, would you guess that more teachers rely on convenient rules or innate gifts? What does your answer suggest for professional development of teachers?

Plus, she uses "classical methods" in new and innovative ways and, thereby, transforms them into personally created individual instruments (MW 9: 177).

Unexpectedly, Dewey claims that general methods of teaching are as relevant to the student and her learning as they are to the teacher and her teaching:

> Part of his learning, a very important part, consists in *becoming* master of the methods which experience of others has shown to be more efficient in like cases of getting knowledge. These general methods are in no way opposed to individual initiative and originality—to personal ways of doing things. On the contrary they are reinforcements of them. For there is a radical difference between even the most general method and a prescribed rule. The latter is a *direct* guide to action; the former operates indirectly through the enlightenment it supplies as to ends and means. It operates, that is to say, through intelligence, and not through conformity to orders externally imposed. (MW 9: 178)

For the teacher and the student, "an animating idea" (MW 9: 178) is needed to qualify them as artists. For it is this idea, end, or goal that inspires and fires the teacher and student and ensures that their teaching and learning—and each is both teacher and learner—are artistically accomplished (MW 9: 178). The teacher uses her intelligence to adapt and modify the known ways of teaching so that she can be effective with each student, personalizing the ideas and techniques, as the student does in her learning. Ultimately, the "constructive value" of the information they have enables them to create different ways of teaching and different ways of learning—different but productive individual styles (MW 9: 178–179).

Second, then, we come to the methods of thinking, learning, and teaching. The "primary factory"—the key element—in general method that experience and research reveal is the scientific method of solving problems—which for Dewey is not the method of a particular science or of the sciences in contrast with, say, the arts or history but reflective thinking—and, hence, reflective teaching and learning (MW 7: 283). Our teaching and learning, in short, should reflect and be shaped by how we think, thus the subtitle of Dewey's book *How We Think* is *A Restatement of the Relation of Reflective Thinking to the Educative Process*. Intelligent problem solving offers insight into how we should design our schools and classrooms, develop our plans and lessons, and select projects and problems. There are many ways we think well and effectively, as there are many others that have not proven successful. The successful ones, Dewey thinks, have things in common. His five steps of this

Table 14.3   The Reflective Thinking Process

Steps	Description
1	A situation arises that clarifies a person's interests and ends and stimulates her desire and effort to reach her goal, typically a problem that prevents life from going on.
2	The conditions arouse the person to notice obstacles and opportunities as she plans to reach her goal.
3	She develops a plan or hypothesis about the best way to reach her goal.
4	The plan is implemented.
5	The anticipated consequences of the plan of action are compared with the actual outcomes, and the plan and hypothesis are evaluated. (MW 7: 283–284)

successful thinking, teaching, and learning are delineated in Table 14.3. Notice that he assumes we are already actively doing things, not sitting around waiting for an occasion to think.

Dewey is adamant about what he describes as "the fundamental question of method in education" (MW 7: 281): The student's consciousness or awareness of the reflective process should follow the unconscious integration of the process into the conditions or environment of the school and classroom. The unconscious assimilation of the reflective attitude and process by students, therefore, should precede their reflection on the attitude and process. To reverse the order may trivialize and make a lock-step procedure out of a freely flowing and discursive method. It risks being meaningless to them because they have no carefully constructed experiences of it on which to draw. In the end, the method of reflection would become an unreflective, affected, contrived, and unproductive charade (MW 7: 281–283). The careful construction of these prior experiences—refining and sharpening what we are naturally inclined to do unreflectively—takes on special importance.

Individual method can now more readily be understood. To begin, Dewey wants us to recognize that "strictly speaking, method is thoroughly individual" (MW 7: 283). General method has to be individualized. Only individuals actually think, and they think in particular cases. The way the teacher uses techniques, software, and materials to cultivate learning are her own, peculiarly and artistically personal. But the student's approach to learning is also her own and, consequently, the issue of teaching method "is ultimately reducible to the question of the order of development of the child's powers and interests" (EW 5: 91). Therefore, to ignore the student in one's creativity isn't sound pedagogy. Neither is ignoring one's own gifts, talents, knowledge, and experience. Accordingly, both teaching and learning ought to be individualized, for "each person has his own instinctive way of going at a thing; the attitude and the mode of approach and attack are individual" (MW 7: 283). Because a teacher's approach to selecting methods that promote reflective learning, her style, is highly personal, it is her responsibility to think imaginatively and creatively about herself and her students as she plans for each student and class.

Although Dewey drops hints and suggestions about specific techniques throughout his writings, we will center our immediate discussion on his observations about those who permanently influenced us the most as teachers. According to him, we remember best those teachers who combined "unity in variety" to create genuine works of art, that is, reflective thinkers who

- connected streams of thought even as they allowed the freedom for reflective diversions;
- mixed originality and methods to sustain our interest and involvement in class and with ideas; and
- used creative and novel methods to focus our attention on fundamental problems and primary topics (LW 8: 155).

He also claims that the teachers we remember doing "the most" for us were people who

- placed us before subjects,
- learned what was going on in our minds,
- discovered our strongest intellectual trait,
- connected our minds with school activities, and
- aroused our intellectual interests so that we grew (LW 17: 224).

The teachers Dewey says we remember are apparently the kind Dewey wishes to support and foster. Undoubtedly, he says, they will have a "characteristic method" of teaching, but they are entitled to "any technical means" that leads to the desired educational results (LW 10: 209). Yet in all the thinking, planning, doing, creating, guiding, questioning, and stimulating that go with her freedom, the teacher remembers that her artistry is a means to facilitate the growth of students (LW 10: 349).

As we might expect of someone so concerned with the art of teaching, Dewey makes a special point of his belief that the image is "the great instrument" (EW 5: 92) of teaching. From his perspective, the student is constantly forming images of school, subjects, teachers, and classmates. Of special importance from an educational stance are the images that she develops of disciplines, subtopics, learning, and education. The teacher should understand each student's images and intervene when appropriate in the learning process to ensure that she is forming "definite, vivid, and growing images" (EW 5: 92). This image-building process involves the student's total learning capacities (e.g., visual, auditory, and motor) and the complete curriculum (LW 17: 242–254).

As we think through the layers of Dewey's thought about the teacher's method, it may be helpful to diagrammatically depict its various dimensions. Table 14.3 synthesizes his ideas and alludes to the importance of intelligence, artistry, and freedom as the teacher works with others to develop multiple methods of educating students.

Now let us turn to our third and final question: How do we evaluate the classroom success of an artist? By what standards do we measure the artistic teacher? This question may seem like a waste of time or, worse, an intrusion into one's artistic freedom. We think, however, that it is important for a number of reasons. Any teacher, for instance, regardless of attitude, performance, and products, may be inclined to think she is free to claim to be a pedagogical artist. This claim might be tolerable if inane in the nonpedagogical arts, but it isn't when we are working with children and youth. Some people, of course, claim they create only for themselves and that others' opinions (which is what they usually call the ideas of others) don't matter. But others believe they can learn from other people's ideas and read reviews and critiques eagerly and attentively, if critically. Perhaps we should see ourselves in the second group, for if we do not do a credible and open job of evaluating our teaching and what goes on in schools, others will do it for us. We have everything to gain by ensuring that we are assessed by people who know something about what we are doing, the challenges we face, and the possibilities open to us.

Another form of our question may be somewhat better: How do we decide whether a teacher is a talented and educated artist and when a person needs considerable development as an artist? How do we determine who the well-developed artists are so that we can learn from them? How do we learn to evaluate our own attitudes and performances to determine what progress we are making in the art of teaching? How do we recognize the art of teaching and the outcomes in our own teaching? Seeking answers to these questions is consistent with Dewey's belief that the art of thinking—which is both a means and an end in classroom teaching—is a "regulative art." That is to say, there is "good thinking and bad thinking" and to teach in ways that foster the former and discourage the latter is the central aim of teachers (MW 12: 158).

As we would expect, Dewey helps us answer our questions. He pens an extended statement that blends together artistic criteria, spirit, technique, vision, and commitment. In all, we identify 17 somewhat commingling criteria that can be used to measure our artistry.

> Now the teacher's own claim to rank as an artist is [1] measured by his ability to foster the attitude of the artist in those who study with him, whether they be youth or little children. Some success [2] in arousing enthusiasm, [3] in communicating large ideas, [4] in evoking energy. So far, well; but the final test is whether the stimulus thus given to wider aims succeeds [5] in transforming itself into power; that is to say, into the attention to detail that ensures mastery over means of execution. If not, [6] zeal flags, [7] the interest dies out, [8] the ideal becomes a clouded memory. Other teachers succeed in training [9] facility, [10] skill, [11] mastery of the technique of subjects. Again it is well—so far. But unless [12] enlargement of mental vision, [13] power of increased discrimination of final values, a sense [14] for ideas, [15] for principles, accompanies this training, forms of skill ready to be put indifferently to any end may be the result. Such modes of technical skill may display themselves, according to circumstances, as cleverness in serving self-interest, as docility in carrying out the purposes of others, or as unimaginative plodding in ruts. To nurture [16] inspiring aim and [17] executive means into harmony with each other is at once the difficulty and the reward of the teacher. (LW 8: 348–349)

Although each of these dispositions and activities is important, three are especially so: (1) "the teacher's . . . ability to foster the attitude of the artist"; (2) "whether the stimulus thus given to wider aims succeeds in transforming itself into power; that is . . . mastery over means of execution"; and (3) "enlargement of mental vision, power of increased discrimination of final values, a sense for ideas, for principles, accompanies this training." Dewey thinks we can distinguish successful classroom artists from those who are less effective. It might be interesting to compare his list—or the three we stress—with contemporary lists of performance indicators and standards of accountability.

QUOTES AND QUESTIONS

In the context of understanding the student's developing purposes, dispositions, inclinations, and abilities, it is important to see what Dewey means when
he asserts that

> the teacher is a trainer of mind, a former of character; . . . an artist above
> nature, yet in harmony with nature, who applies the science of education
> to help another to the full realization of his personality in a character
> of strength, beauty, freedom—to say this is simply to proclaim that the
> problem of education is essentially an ethical and psychological problem.
> (Archambault, 1964, p. 197)

In this statement, Dewey identifies the teacher as a trainer, a former, and
an artist above nature. What do you think he means by the last phrase? What
is the connection to the teacher's activities being in accord with the student's nature? Does his thought allow for individual method? How can the problem of education be largely both ethical and psychological? Why would he make this claim when he is noted for saying that many disciplines contribute to a science or theory of education?

> **An Introspective Moment**
>
> When you think about your teaching, is it largely trial-and-error based or principle based? Who do you know that seems to base her practice on principles drawn from carefully examined theory, research, and reflection? Can you talk with her about your interest in educational principles?

That Dewey discourages a recipe, rules of thumb, trial-and-error methods, and unreflective approaches to
teaching is abundantly clear. He wants methods of teaching to be selected in
light of what it means to be an artist, the nature and abilities of each student,
the disciplines that enlighten educational theory, and the wisdom of practitioners. But he also thinks technique is a personal matter for each teacher. How
do we reconcile, if we can, these ideas with another of his beliefs: "There is a
technique of teaching, just as there is a technique of piano-playing. The technique if it is to be educationally effective, is dependent upon principles" (MW
3: 254)? Can the artist's method or technique be both personal and based on
principles? Is he implying that there are some common principles on which

teaching ought to be based? If so, what do you think are the most important ones? Are these common principles part of an educational theory?

IMPLICATIONS FOR THE TEACHER

Dewey's thinking about the attitude, method, and measure of the artistic teacher has many significant implications. Clearly, Dewey thinks that the passion that drives the teacher's activities and sets her goals is extremely important. Without an artistic spirit, the teacher is unlikely to influence student learning and growth and see spirit energizing classroom activities. Activities, projects, problems, and ideas aren't sufficiently compelling if the navigator is dozing. Is feeding our souls, our total beings, then, as important as nourishing our professional minds? Ironically, art, in all of its variety, can help us do this. To paraphrase Dewey, what has a teacher gained if she knows everything about students, neighborhoods, teaching, classroom management, parental interests, subject matter, technology, and educational materials and loses her own soul (LW 13: 29)?

Equally clear is Dewey's belief that general educational methods—the conditions of the classroom—can be a potent ally of the teacher, the most powerful influence for learning. When a school pays attention to them, each student, teacher, counselor, aide, custodian, cook, volunteer, and administrator is contributing to a learning environment: the school and classroom. The science or knowledge to use in building these conditions already exists to a sizable degree. As artistic teachers, we can use this knowledge to increase our effectiveness. To paraphrase Dewey again, what has a teacher gained if she undertakes each learning activity with compassion, brilliance, and beauty but loses her pedagogical effectiveness by ignoring the broader classroom and school conditions?

Finally, it will probably be more helpful to reflect on Dewey's ideas about measuring our success as artistic teachers and tease out their relevance with others than to do so by ourselves. Creative people interacting with one another have much to share and learn. Our experiential knowledge—so seldom valued and shared in formal ways—shouldn't be ignored, least of all by us. To paraphrase Dewey, what has a teacher gained if she learns from the greatest minds, books, articles, materials, software, and websites of the world and loses the wisdom offered by her colleagues and her own experience?

A SUMMATIVE EXERCISE

Chapter 14   The Teacher as Classroom Teacher

Understandings	Qualities	Activities

READINGS

"The Educational Balance, Efficiency and Thinking," (LW 17: 77–82).
"Imagination," (LW 17: 242–254).
"Method," (MW 7: 277–284).
"Native Resources in Training Thought," in *How We Think* (LW 8: 35–54).
"The Nature of Method," in *Democracy and Education* (MW 9: 171–187).
"School Conditions and the Training of Thought," in *How We Think* (LW 8: 55–68).

FIFTEEN

Conclusion

We may look forward, therefore, to a society in which teachers are fairly secure and truly free. We can hope that they will be encouraged to attack professional problems in a creative spirit. We foresee the kind of administration which exalts the free and intelligent personality and does not depend upon rules, regulations, formal procedures, and prescriptions. Under these conditions teaching can become the high art that it rarely is today. Teachers individually and in their professional organizations can develop standards without being hampered by external worries, limited economic resources, impossible working conditions, military-minded executives, and popular misunderstanding of the function and work of schools.

—John Dewey (LW 11: 546)

The rather optimistic theme of this vision that Dewey coauthors—a time when teachers will be free professionals in a democratic

Authors' Note: References to works by John Dewey are from the collection of his works published by Southern Illinois University Press: *The Early Works of John Dewey, 1882–1898; The Middle Works of John Dewey, 1899–1924;* and *The Later Works of John Dewey, 1925–1953.* References to these works are abbreviated as EW, MW, and LW, where, for example, EW 5: 94 indicates that the material cited or idea noted is in *The Early Works,* Volume 5, page 94.

society—suggests his faith in human potential and those who play significant roles in its development. Sadly, his prophetic gifts are less well developed than his hopes, dreams, and faith. Even so, he is probably not much different than most of us. Our hopes for the future, our students, schools, and society remain firm in the face of limited overall progress and, at times, educational setbacks. Without such hope, however, we will surely be less enthusiastic servants and artists as we pursue the education of children and youth and the development of society. Our ideals are important in sustaining us as professionals—and as people. The day our ideals, hopes, and faith die is the day our loves and passions depart and the day we should consider another line of work.

Does it matter that Dewey is not an accurate prophet? In one sense, no, for it is much more important to have a positive spirit and vision than to be accurate all of the time. Or, we could say, to have a hopeful outlook as we pursue our many ideals is a great deal more important than arriving at a particular destination. But arriving at some of our destinations is extremely important for students and society and immensely rewarding for us. Thus, it is important that we recognize and remember the progressive steps we make with each of our students. Student progress is an invaluable foundation stone for building and enhancing their individual and collective futures, our profession, and society. The positive mind and the hopeful spirit, therefore, should not be undervalued or underestimated. Being happy about the educative growth of our students is a strong motivating force and helps keep our dreams and faith alive. As we blend student progress, professional hope, and pedagogical artistry, we increase the probability that teaching, learning, and living will become more characterized by aesthetic experiences.

Behind this prophecy, then, may be an ideal that is looked forward to, hoped for, and worked for. As a dynamic end, it is alive and growing. As we take steps toward it, we gain greater clarity of what we can and should be doing and how we can continue to pursue our vision. When educational, social, and political support exists for our ideal, our excitement about the future can grow. When this support is inadequate, it may be helpful to read some educational history, especially of the evolving roles and responsibilities of teachers. In that history, we find grounds for believing that in the long view, progress as a profession and as a democracy is being made. This is not to say that much work doesn't remain or that we can be satisfied with where we are, but if we keep working toward our ideals, present crises and disasters may well pass.

Thinking about the negative images that Dewey mentions may also be useful, for example, followers of blueprints, living phonographs, rubber stamps, cogs in machines, servants of privileged classes, factory employees, magistrates, hostages of the fortunate, perfunctory instructors, conduits of information, dictators, and negligible factors. Compare these with positive images: artists, lovers, wise mothers, navigators, gardeners, pioneers, physicians, farmers, engineers, chefs, social servants, guides, midwives, learning co-partners, curriculum builders, composers, judges, nurses, intellectual leaders, and orchestral conductors. In a sense, the former set of images is imposed on us; the latter is created by us. Choice, however constrained, is still alive in schools. Not even the military-minded administrators that Dewey mentions can completely take it from us.

The sharp contrast we see between these two image collections may serve other purposes. First, it may provide us with the inspiration to strive for the positive world and not to accept the negative one that some wish to impose on us. Each of us individually and all of us collectively have a voice, however small, in whether we will be perceived as servants of privileged classes or servants of democratic ideas, cogs in machines or chefs in fine restaurants, conduits of information or conductors of symphonies. This point isn't a romantic ideal to be lost on our psyches but a reality that can be continuously pursued by professionals.

> **A Teacher Snapshot**
>
> As you think back through Dewey's images, which teacher do you know who best exhibits the qualities of the largest number of them? What were her greatest strengths?

Second, as we think of ourselves in positive ways, our thoughts can eventually influence our feelings and behaviors. Certainly, feeding ourselves on the psychological porridge that emanates from those who distribute "rules, regulations, formal procedures, and prescriptions" (LW 11: 546) won't help us change. We must, as Dewey argues, move beyond positive words and thoughts to behavior or actions. As even Dewey says, there is such a thing as thinking too much. Thinking that doesn't lead to appropriate action is excessive and wasteful (LW 8: 147).

Third, if our interpretation is correct, most of us are somewhere between the two ends of the continuum, between followers of blueprints and composers of aesthetic experiences. The ideologies of some business leaders, government officials, and different publics push us at times toward the negative end. Ideally, intelligent voices—including our own—will push back each time ideologies seek to discredit, if not destroy, public schools and teachers. As a group, we need to be committed to promoting the ongoing progress of the profession in the face of counterproductive forces. As professionals, we should contribute to the positive stream of thought and practice that Dewey paints if we intend to remain the artistic servants of a free society.

Fourth, the positive set of images that Dewey provides may give us a small edge in attracting and retaining more artistically talented teachers. The greater our numbers and the greater our support system, the greater our positive influence can become. Maximizing our potential for education, democracy, and artistry is enhanced if we recruit, not the best and brightest minds, but the best people to become talented classroom artists. We hope—and have faith—that this will be the outcome, but we are in need of much more than recruitment and retention efforts if we are going to maximize our influence. How shall we further maximize our strength for democratic and educative schools?

Fifth, if we look back at the epigraph, we may find another implication for helping to build better schools. We should reconsider the potential for good that rests in the hands and hearts of reflective, humane, and democratically oriented school and district administrators. Administrators ought to be—and often are—the allies of schools where freedom, creativity, intelligence, and problem solving are valued. Also, they should be educators who seek to protect teachers from an environment becoming increasingly dominated by rules, procedures, and directives. In short, we need administrators who as teachers were and who in their new responsibilities are artists, lovers, wise mothers, navigators, gardeners, pioneers, physicians, engineers, chefs, social servants, guides, midwives, group leaders, curriculum builders, composers, judges, nurses, intellectual leaders, and orchestral conductors.

The positive images, therefore, may help us attract future administrators who are practicing pedagogical artists and who plan to become practicing administrative artists. Their methods will be informed by their ideals, artistic spirit joined with collegial respect, experimental attitude united with cooperative relationships, creative inclinations accompanied by participatory practices, and pedagogical passions married to administrative responsibilities. If not, they will encourage teachers to be disinterested, unconcerned, passive, indifferent, evasive, and—we hope—rebellious (LW 11: 224ff; LW 11: 343ff).

Rebellious, we hope, because there are few other options to keeping the artistic spirit alive when working in an educational death camp. Or, as Dewey says on a related theme:

> Without light, a people perishes. Without freedom, light grows dim and darkness comes to reign. Without freedom, old truths become so stale and worn that they cease to be truths and become mere dictates of external authority. Without freedom, search for new truth and the disclosure of new paths in which humanity may walk more securely and justly come to an end. (LW 11: 254)

Although he understands the multiple tensions, contradictory demands, and enormous pressures felt by administrators, Dewey does not leave us without hope regarding school leadership. Instead, he encourages administrators to integrate their three major responsibilities—education, personal relationships, and routine and mechanical matters—and to decide that they will not capitulate or conform to external or internal pressures to deemphasize their most important duty, that is, providing support for educative experiences. Their commitment to this responsibility includes a choice to support adult education, for without it the education of children and youth is compromised:

> The administrator will conceive adult education to be a necessary part of his job, not in the sense of providing adult classes and lectures—helpful as these may be—but in the sense that only as the public is brought to understand the needs and possibilities of the creative education of the young, can education be vitally effective. He will realize that public education is essentially education *of* the public: directly, through teachers and students in the school; indirectly, through communicating to others his own ideals and standards, inspiring others with the enthusiasm of himself and his staff for the function of intelligence and character in the transformation of society. (LW 11: 347)

Administrators, on the other hand, are not alone in this responsibility to educate the public. We need to take advantage of opportunities as well as create them as we engage in education of the public. Can we passively watch as society sends antieducative wave after wave at schools? Hardly. Realizing the connection of society to schools and the need for well-educated and responsible citizens who develop educative environments that are external to schools, he turns to teachers and asks us to "bear a responsibility as leaders, as directors in the formation of public opinion" (MW 7: 110).

In truth, however, we know that some community leaders and board members do not desire a genuinely democratic society or school and want exactly what students and schools don't need: administrators who are followers of blueprints and rubber stamps. This preference by some highly influential people presents another challenge and brings us to another idea that emerges from thinking about the continuum of the cog and the chef.

So, sixth, if we have an image of the kind of educational administrators who ought to be appointed, we should consider encouraging people with complementary philosophies and values to prepare to be principals and superintendents. Leaving the selection of administrators entirely or largely in the hands of those who are simply attracted—with the wide range of motives that are associated with positional desirability—to administration isn't necessarily wise, either. A person attracted to administration—and the same could be said of people attracted to teaching—may have values that are antithetical to creative, educative, reflective, and artistic environments. Being proactive and encouraging educational artists to think about becoming administrators is at least worthy of reflection.

A Reflective Opportunity

Being either an artistic principal or an artistic teacher is an immensely challenging position. What teachers and principals do you recall who combined their arts to make schools creative, experimental, and effective learning communities? Do you know how these communities evolved?

Of course, the input of parents, administrative staff, and board members is also critical. If parents, staff, and board members wish to, they can frequently find and employ candidates or applicants who will promote uniformity, standardization, and regulation. This fact suggests a seventh responsibility—alluded to in part earlier—for those us who want to practice our art in a professional atmosphere. The epigraph helps if we use our imaginations once again: Professional organizations of teachers can develop standards not just for being classroom artists, but for the selection of future administrative artists. Why should we leave the development of these sets of standards primarily or entirely up to those who see through bureaucratic, authoritarian, and regulatory lenses? This is not to say that policymakers and administrators are *ipso facto* the enemies of classroom artistry. Many are intelligent, creative, and caring. Nor is it to say that all teachers will be great administrators. Dewey rightly reminds us that teachers are not necessarily free of the desire to be educational lords, rulers, and judges (LW 2: 58–59).

On the other hand, those who have been imaginative and democratic teachers may continue to display these qualities as educational leaders. But we are less than straightforward if we don't admit that a sizable number of administrators are not the friends of lively, experimental, and flexible teaching and learning. Proportionately, their numbers may be no larger than the number of wooden teachers we have, but their influence is much greater, affecting a wider range of students, teachers, and the public. We need neither wooden teachers nor bureaucratic administrators, and we don't need the former becoming the latter.

Teacher association statements about the qualities of democratic educational leaders can serve at least a threefold purpose: (1) to inform aspiring administrators of the ideals and expectations of those with whom they may work with in the future, (2) to remind existing administrators of the vision of leadership that classroom teachers have, and (3) to raise the consciousness level of those who make personnel recommendations and decisions. These statements can emphasize that we want colleagues who share our values and visions, respect our expertise as practitioners, and encourage pedagogical artistry in schools.

In this regard, we might borrow and modernize a few of Dewey's ideas as we ask for administrators who will help teachers, students, caregivers, and others:

- build schools and classrooms that are genuine learning communities;
- promote students' social and personal growth as educated citizens;
- develop school curricula that value students' prior learning experiences;
- understand each student outside and in school environments;
- study neighborhoods and cultures to align the community and the school curriculum;
- foster an artistic spirit in the school community;
- create aesthetic learning experiences for all students;
- cultivate students' understanding of facts, interpretations, and ideas as tools for thinking about and solving problems;
- promote independent thinking and social responsibility among students and teachers;
- expect and treat others with respect;

- operate on the principle that each student and teacher is unique;
- use their imaginations in thinking, learning, and teaching; and
- encourage courageous and experimental approaches to teaching and learning.

We could add that, above all, we want administrators who help us create climates in which lists like this are no longer needed.

In short, we've talked about what being an artistic teacher entails and the kinds of environments that are needed in classrooms and schools. We also noted the importance of having administrators who support and lead schools that provide educative and aesthetic experiences. Such schools provide a better education for children and youth but also indirectly help build a better society for everyone. Yet, a society that sends attack after attack of antieducative policies, expectations, practices, and restraints at these educational islands will erode its good schools and prevent new ones from being built. Schools, certainly, are not the whole answer. Rhetoric that suggests they are is off-putting at best. Policy that implies that they are only undermines legitimate ways of solving problems. Schools cannot solve all society's problems. Indeed, they cannot solve even the majority of them. The school is only one educative source. "Every place" that children, youth, and adults gather is "perforce a school-house," and these other schools can collectively do great harm if not attended to by society (MW 7: 304).

Unless citizens—including board members, parents, politicians, and others—build supportive larger cultures or environments, the damage caused by these "other schools" can be substantial, if not immeasurable.

Realizing the connection of society to schools and the need for well-educated, responsible citizens who develop educative environments outside of schools, Dewey says:

> What teachers do as citizens in supporting or failing to support the movements which endeavor to protect or to extend democracy may also contribute, even more than usual classroom practice, to the realization of a better society and a consequently better education. Teachers may, however, play a more understanding and more enthusiastic part in the contemporary social struggle if they appreciate the kind of education which may result from the victory of democracy. (LW 11: 547)

Whether Dewey should ask us to accept this challenge is open to debate. Whether our influence is needed isn't. But let's not be simply pedagogues who are "only too willing to talk and write and argue about things" (MW 7: 87). Moreover, let's not forget that we are more than teachers. We are also citizens who may more passionately protect and extend democracy if we recognize the value of "the kind of education which may result from the victory of democracy" (LW 11: 547). With progressive victories of democracy in the political, governmental, judicial, institutional, economic, and social phases of life, we will be progressively establishing the conditions for teaching to become "the high art" needed (LW 11: 217ff).

READINGS

"Democracy and Educational Administration," (LW 11: 217–225).
"Freedom," (LW 11: 247–255).
"The Need for Orientation," (LW 11: 162–166).
"The Teacher and the Public," (LW 11: 158–161).
"Toward Administrative Statesmanship," (LW 11: 345–347).

Index

Plato, 8
Playfulness, mental, 193–194
Problem solving
    appropriate problems
        for, 169
    authentic problems
        for, 169
    learning cycle and,
        165–167
    teaching methods and,
        197–198
    thinking and, 34
Professional development
    role of reflection in,
        124–125
    understanding cultural
        background of students
        through, 150–151
Psychology, 31
Public, need for educating,
    211, 214–215

The Quest for Certainty, 34
Questioning. *See* Inquiry

*Reconstruction in
    Philosophy*, 45
Reflection
    educational contribution
        of, 119–122
    open-mindedness, 180–181
    process of, 198
    See also Inquiry; Thinking
Reform, piecemeal, 154
Rousseau, Jean-Jacques, 8

Salesperson, teacher
    as, 66–67
School
    as community, 45–46
    conditions of, 194–196
    democracy and, 81–82, 100,
        102–105, 107–110
    hostility to genuine
        experiences of,
        130–131
    influence on individual of,
        69, 91–92, 214
    social role of, 81–82
The School and Society
    child's impulses, 149
    on educational value of
        home, 44

Science, and education, 93–94,
    117–119. *See also*
    Educational theory
Self-criticism, 124
Servant, teacher as.
    See Social service
Social engineer, teacher as,
    115–125
Social service
    education as promoting,
        19, 21–22
    leadership and, 186
    love of others and,
        31–32, 37
    teacher role in, 99–110
*The Sources of a Science of
    Education*, 116–118,
    122, 125
Students
    character building, 168–169,
        171–172
    democracy as personal way
        of life for, 109
    development of, 77–80,
        82–83, 151–154
    early human impulses of,
        149–154
    environmental influences
        on, 43–47, 75,
        150–151, 164–165
    experience and, 129–142
    products of teacher's art,
        36–38, 51–52, 202. *See
        also* character building
    role in learning of, 59–61,
        63–64
    souls of, 147–157
    starting point of education,
        74–77, 150–151
    teacher-student relationship,
        23, 30–32, 147–157
    teacher study of, 74–77, 156
Subject matter, teacher love
    for, 33–34
Supervision of teachers, 170

Teacher education programs
    as educational resource,
        65, 68
    role of reflection in, 120
Teachers
    characteristics of, 23–24,
        30–38, 91, 193–194

constructive activities
    of, 161–172
education and knowledge
    of, 161
effective, 199
evaluation of, 200–201
future for, 207–215
job duties of, 4
leadership by, 177–186
modeling of behaviors for
    students, 24
moral responsibilities of,
    182–184
motivations of, 29–36
natural, 33
pressures on, 147–148, 172
recruitment and retention
    of, 210
role in student learning of,
    59–61, 63–64, 177–186
student-teacher relationship,
    23, 30–32, 147–157
techniques of, 194, 199
time allocation by, 172
Teaching
    authentic experience and,
        140–142
    difficulty of, 4–6, 14–15
    teacher-directed learning, 75
Theory of education.
    See Educational theory
Thinking
    aesthetic experience, 142
    as art, 68
    open-minded, 180–181
    reflective, 197–199
    teacher love for, 34–35
    unproductive, 178–180
    See also Inquiry;
        Reflection
Time, instructional, 172
"To a Pedant" (poem), 93
"To Those Who Aspire
    to the Profession of
    Teaching," 29
Tradition, 116, 123–124

Watson, Goodwin, 162
Wisdom, 53
Wise mother, teacher as,
    43–50
Wise physician, teacher
    as, 147–157

Printed in the United States
49684LVS00004B/10